# SUGARCANE AND RUM

JOHN R. GUST
and JENNIFER P. MATHEWS

# SUGAR CANE & RUM

The Bittersweet History of Labor and
Life on the Yucatán Peninsula

THE UNIVERSITY OF
ARIZONA PRESS
TUCSON

The University of Arizona Press
www.uapress.arizona.edu

ISBN-13: 978-0-8165-3888-1 (paper)

Cover design by Derek Thornton, Notch Design
Cover art: *Construction of the Palace of Cortes* [detail]. Rivera, Diego (1886–1957) Credit: Photo
© Luisa Ricciarini/Bridgeman Images

Publication was made possible in part by funding from Trinity University's Academic Affairs
office.

Library of Congress Cataloging-in-Publication Data
Names: Gust, John R., 1978– author. | Mathews, Jennifer P., 1969– author.
Title: Sugarcane and rum : the bittersweet history of labor and life on the Yucatán Peninsula /
    John R. Gust and Jennifer P. Mathews.
Description: Tucson, Arizona : The University of Arizona Press, 2020. | Includes bibliographi-
    cal references and index.
Identifiers: LCCN 2019046941 | ISBN 9780816538881 (paperback)
Subjects: LCSH: Agricultural laborers—Yucatán Peninsula—Social conditions—19th century.
    | Agricultural laborers—Yucatán Peninsula—History—19th century. | Mayas—Yucatán
    Peninsula—Social conditions—19th century. | Mayas—Yucatán Peninsula—History—19th
    century. | Sugarcane industry—Mexico—History—19th century. | Rum industry—Mex-
    ico—History—19th century.
Classification: LCC F1435.3.A37 G87 2020 | DDC 305.897/427—dc23
LC record available at https://lccn.loc.gov/2019046941

*This book is dedicated to our mentor, Scott L. Fedick.*

# CONTENTS

# ILLUSTRATIONS

## FIGURES

## MAPS

## TABLES

# ACKNOWLEDGMENTS

ALTHOUGH WE EARNED OUR DEGREES eighteen years apart, we were brought together by our shared advisor, Scott Fedick. We are so thankful for his mentorship, friendship, and all the opportunities he has provided us. This book is the culmination of nearly a decade of research into a fascinating period in Quintana Roo, a place that we have grown to love as much for the people as for the archaeology. Our fieldwork involved many days in dusty archives, long rides in the Combi that mostly got us where we needed to be, boat rides through a beautiful lagoon, surveys through the mangroves, and a lot of mosquitoes.

We conducted all archaeological research under permits granted by the Instituto Nacional de Antropologia e Historia (INAH), and we especially want to recognize the staff of the Quintana Roo office of the INAH for all their help. We are also grateful to the staff of the General Archives in Yucatán (Archivo General del Estado de Yucatán, AGEY) for their patience as we picked through their collection. This research could not have been completed without the aid of the staffs of the Trinity University Department of Sociology and Anthropology (in particular, Kate Schubert) and the University of California, Riverside, Department of Anthropology. The internal review boards at both of these universities supported us asking interesting questions of the inhabitants of the Yalahau region while ensuring they were not harmed by our investigations. The unsung heroes of every research project are the librarians (like Alex Gallin-Parisi) and especially those working in the interlibrary loan offices. We also thank Karin and Eric Vonk for inviting us to visit Richland Rum, and distiller Roger Zimmerman for answering our endless questions. We extend our gratitude to Stephanie Croatt for all her help and enthusiasm in the early days of this project, and to Lucia Gudiel for her assistance in the soil laboratory.

We thank the people of the Yalahau region—especially those who guided our trips to Xuxub, Rancho Aznar, and San Eusebio, and the folks from Cuzuma who showed us their Decauville rail system. Thanks also go to Mitch Cocom for all his help in and out of the field.

We must also thank our colleagues who made this project possible. We are so grateful to Paul Sullivan, who, at the beginning of this project, so generously gave us access to his research documents and notes on Xuxub, which helped us frame our initial research questions. Many thanks to Jeffrey Glover and Dominique Rissolo for being our project directors, collaborators, and always our friends. Thank you to our friend Charles "Bush" Bush, who provided us with years of research support and who always gave us a place to stay when we came to the beach to recharge. Thank you to the brilliant Macduff Everton for so graciously sharing your incredible photographs for use in this book, as they greatly enhance it. We are also deeply indebted to the anonymous peer reviewers who provided insightful comments and made this an infinitely better book through the process, and to our editor Allyson Carter, Scott De Herrera, and the staff at the University of Arizona Press, who so ably shepherded this project through.

Lastly, we would like to thank our loved ones for their support through this project. John thanks Lauren Schwartz for listening as he worked through ideas and for watching superhero movies with him when he needed a break. Jennifer thanks her husband, Marco Martinez, for making her morning coffee every day, for his patience as she put in long days on the laptop, and for always being there with a hug, kiss, and a smile at the end of the day.

# SUGARCANE AND RUM

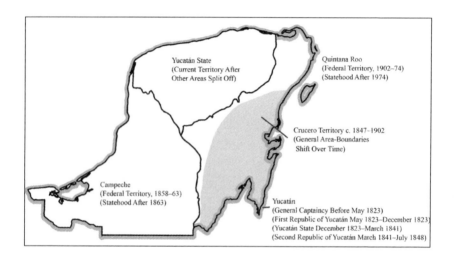

**MAP 1.** Mexican Yucatán as constituted over time. (Map by John R. Gust.)

# INTRODUCTION

WHILE THE STORY OF SUGARCANE and rum production in the Caribbean has been told many times, and in many ways, few know the bittersweet story of sugar and rum in the jungles of the Yucatán Peninsula (map 1) during the nineteenth century.[1] Because this story is quite distinct, as a mode of comparison in chapter 1, we start by telling the better-known history of sugar and rum in the New World in Barbados, Jamaica, Hispaniola (Haiti and the Dominican Republic), Trinidad, Brazil, Cuba, and the United States. What this history shows is that sugarcane and rum are produced on a massive scale to satisfy the consumptive needs of the colonizers, which only compounds its exploitative nature as the products become available to the middle and working class.

In chapter 2, we compare the different systems of coercive labor used in sugar-producing regions. In the rest of the Americas, sugarcane was tied to the slave trade more than any other commodity. Sugar and rum were highly profitable when sold in Europe and often used as payment for enslaved persons in Africa. The system became known as the *triangular trade*, resulting in a dependency on a coerced labor force that placed Europeans in precarious positions vis-à-vis the world economy. We briefly examine case studies of colonization and slavery in the Americas to better understand how workers fought to be free while their employers coerced them into various states of "unfreedom."

In the Yucatán Peninsula of México, however, sugarcane used the debt peonage system rather than relying on imported slaves. While it borrowed elements from feudalism and slavery, it also co-opted elements of labor service that were historically expected from Maya residents for the betterment of their communities.[2] Employers gave debt peons loans that both parties understood were unlikely to ever be repaid, and as debt grew, the workers' freedoms were increasingly curtailed. Once deeply indebted, workers needed permission to leave the hacienda at all.[3] Maya workers had few paths to exit peonage but were often adept at taking full advantage of their few avenues for maintaining any autonomy they had while pushing back against their employer's worst abuses. The debt peons could drag their feet, demand an accounting of debts to see if another employer would buy them out, and use the legal system (even if Indigenous testimony was given less weight by the courts) to combat abuses that went too far.[4] These and other "weapons of the weak" often had negative consequences but were nonetheless available strategies.[5]

Peonage also had benefits in that workers gained access to farmland, funds for weddings and other rites of passage, and a paternal safety net during times of environmental crisis, or for when they were too old to work. They gained the stability that landless Maya unattached to haciendas did not have, but at the cost of their independence.[6] From the employer perspective, debt peons represented an investment, while the day laborer was disposable. The only other option for many was to work as day laborers, which was usually only available at the "crunch" times of planting and harvest. Because employers saw day laborers as disposable, these proletarians lived a particularly precarious existence that has recently been dubbed the "precariat."[7]

An important distinction between Yucatán and the rest of the sugar-producing world was that planters in Yucatán did not engage directly with the world system as sellers of sugar and rum, because they were not producing enough surplus for export. This was in part because Yucatán suffered from the tumultuous internal politics of the Spanish Empire and social strife, leaving it unable to meet its own demand. However, sugar and rum producers did engage with the world as importers of tools and technologies. Growers imported machines like sugar grinders from the United States and brought expertise from other sugar-producing regions.[8] Haciendas also engaged in competition on a local scale, often trying to outdo each other with improved access to infrastructure or through sabotage.[9]

In contrast, planters in European colonies were subject to the strictures imposed on them by their home governments and were there for the benefit of that empire. They were also subject to reduced sale prices due to competition between colonies, high tariffs on goods imported to the colonies, and export duties that increased sharply if sugar was fully refined prior to export.[10] Home countries claimed to use these taxes to defray the cost of protecting the colonies.[11] Smugglers also took advantage of offering untaxed goods at prices well below those of legal goods while still collecting a healthy profit.[12] Taxes imposed on the American colonies, who lacked representation in British Parliament, helped incite the American Revolution.[13]

As we discuss in chapter 3, laws enforced in the rest of the Spanish Empire regulating the export of sugar-derived products were irrelevant in Yucatán. Instead, in response to complaints of labor shortages from producers of other agricultural products, the Crown limited the amount of sugar that could be produced and outlawed rum distillation in Yucatán. Another potential factor was the Crown's limitations on the amount of forced labor that Indigenous peoples could be compelled to complete. After Mexican independence was realized in 1821, these limitations were no longer in place, and Yucatán developed into a plantocracy.[14] Chapter 3 also extends our discussion of rum production and labor relations on Yucatecan haciendas to an exploration of how rum impacted daily life under this new planter class. Henequen (sisal) hacienda workers were major consumers of much of the rum (aguardiente) produced in the region, as it was served at events such as weddings, sold at company stores, and sometimes paid to itinerant workers in lieu of cash. To the hacienda owner, or hacendado, providing this rum to workers was an important means of indebting them by starting a cycle of debt peonage that entrapped the worker, their spouse, and future generations of their family.[15]

Chapter 4 details the story of how northeastern Quintana Roo became the focus of sugar and rum production. In the three decades preceding the turn of the twentieth century, Yucatán state was one of the wealthiest regions of México due to the export of henequen fiber to the United States, primarily for use as bailing twine.[16] However, Quintana Roo's environment could not support this crop, and planters turned instead to sugarcane. Gust has remarked that no one with other options would choose to work on a sugar hacienda, as it is hard, dangerous, and poorly compensated work.[17] Archaeologically, the sugar industry in the Yucatán Peninsula suffers from "invisibility" in several ways. To begin with, although the sites are less than 150 years old, they contain few artifacts. A majority of the metal artifacts and infrastructure has been removed and likely recycled or sold for scrap. In addition, because of the remote location of our sites in the mangrove swamps of northern Quintana Roo, there are few archival sources available. This region had a dearth of churches, and thus we lack a number of the usual birth, death, and marriage records, and we have located only a handful of relevant labor records. Finally, women and children were integral in supporting the labor of men but are absent archaeologically or in the few labor records we have located. Thus we have a relatively "thin" archaeological and historical record to work with, and we have turned to historical comparison and ethnographic interviews to help us fill in some of these blanks. For example, we have turned to the better preserved and more widely documented henequen haciendas of the same period in Yucatán state to help provide insight. Henequen hacienda operations act as a point of comparison for understanding labor relations, infrastructure, and production in the sugarcane and rum industry. In a recursive way, to understand the henequen hacienda, we must understand rum, and to understand rum, we must understand the henequen hacienda.

Furthermore, in chapter 4 we argue that sugar and rum production in Yucatán were influenced by two major factors: (1) the growing cycle that affected when and how much labor was needed, and (2) the social relationship between the owner and working class that influenced where sugar was produced. Sugarcane cultivation and sugar production moved from the central and southeastern portions of the peninsula to the wilds of the northeastern coast as a result of the uneven end of the Caste War of Yucatán. The authors' work investigating the small site of San Antonio Xuxub (hereafter Xuxub) and the larger site of San Eusebio near the northeastern coast of Yucatán provides details of daily life at sugar haciendas along the northeast coast of Yucatán.[18] One thing that is not determined by where the sugarcane was grown is that working sugar is a brutal way to make a living that few would do willingly, in Yucatán or elsewhere.

In chapter 5, we investigate how the legal and social framework surrounding the production, sale, and consumption of rum was integral to the functioning of the Yucatecan economy. We see the development of the *cantina* in urban centers like Mérida, resulting in changing social mores. Although intoxicating beverages were well integrated within the ritual drinking rites in Mesoamerican societies, rum and other distilled beverages with high alcohol content were unknown to the people of the New World.[19] While chicha (corn beer) and pulque were used in ritual contexts, the Maya (and Mexicans, more generally) began drinking rum in these new social spaces.[20] Yucatán's cantinas were raucous places, where workers could lose their inhibitions and have access to sex workers, thus also providing needed, if low status and potentially dangerous, work for women. These spaces increased the rate of alcohol-fueled incidents, including domestic violence.

We also look at how rum continues to impact Yucatán today through the cases of the Maya Riviera and the Mérida area by showing how the current economies of these areas are predicated on the rum-influenced local social systems of the past. This chapter discusses the ways that tourism in Cancún and the Maya Riviera similarly obscures things such as the living conditions of workers and the stressors placed on the local environment. In the Mexican state of Yucatán, tourists stay in the heart of the capital in Mérida, drawn by its museums, cathedrals, and rich colonial history that echoes of the hacienda's past. They experience a bustling city life; walk among working people, vendors, and traffic jams; and eat Yucatecan cuisine. In the adjacent state of Quintana Roo, the city of Cancún has a decidedly different character and is intentionally designed as an escapist destination. From the Cancún airport, there is a direct road to the near shore island that has been developed into the Hotel Zone that avoids gritty downtown Cancún. A bridge connects the island with picturesque views of the Caribbean Sea to the north and the mangrove river (ria) to the south. The Mexican government transformed this sleepy island into a tourist center with luxury hotels, chain restaurants like TGI Fridays, nightclubs, and high-end malls. The tourist zone's hotels and all-inclusive resorts cater to spring breakers who want to be on vacation from learning and life, and do not want to see the problems of downtown Cancún. The resorts are made to be easy for the amateur U.S. traveler with limited vacation days, so they accept U.S. dollars, the staff speak English, and trips around the area are planned extensively so tourists can be uninvolved in making decisions on their vacation.

Besides the physical separation of the Hotel Zone from downtown, this obfuscation is furthered in other ways. The city has passed laws that clear the tourist areas of beggars and established separate tourist markets that are too expensive for locals to frequent.[21] Although buyers may find the occasional wooden mask or figurine produced in the Yucatán Peninsula, they are more likely to see central Mexican sombreros, T-shirts emblazoned with Cancún on the front and an Aztec calendar on the back, or tchotchkes made in China. The interaction between tourists and hotel workers is meant to be limited. Some hotels and resorts have vans and buses emblazoned with company logos that shuttle employees to and from work in company uniforms. These shuttles play a dual role in providing employees transportation to work while preserving the look of the hotel or resort.[22] Maids are expected to clean the hotel rooms when guests are at the beach, and all aspects of service are relegated to areas out of sight.[23] Even food is distinguished from the local cuisine in the Hotel Zone. In addition to the placement of a high number of U.S. chain restaurants on the island, chefs in tourist hotels and restaurants generally avoid locally caught fish and locally grown produce due to perceived aesthetic and quality issues. While hotels and restaurants could, with minimal investment, help increase local food production capability, few such programs have been initiated.[24] Lastly, the Cancún Hotel Zone distinguishes itself by being one of the only locations in México where foreign tourists can legally purchase alcohol on election day.

This book explores how rum has touched and still touches most parts of Yucatecan life and society, sometimes in subtle ways. In the eighteenth and nineteenth centuries, the economies of many Caribbean islands were organized around the production of sugar. In contrast, our argument for the importance of rum in Yucatán is based on the breadth of the connections more so than seeing the effects of rum and sugar production as totalizing. During the late nineteenth and early twentieth centuries, Yucatán was México's richest region because of the export of henequen to the United States. Rum was instrumental in securing a cheap and plentiful workforce on haciendas. Hacendados loaned their peons money to purchase rum for celebrations such as weddings or even paid bar tabs from cantina owners.[25] While drunk, many workers beat their family members, resulting in pain and a deep distrust of alcohol consumption within many small communities. By looking at the history of sugarcane and rum production through various perspectives, we hope to reveal an untold history and shed light on the significant influence these commodities had on daily life in Yucatán.

# CHAPTER 1

# SUGAR AND RUM PRODUCTION IN THE AMERICAS

THE TALE OF RUM IS woven within the history of the colonialist sugar trade during the "Age of Discovery." One irony is that sugarcane, a plant that is native to and domesticated in the Old World, went on to affect the history of the New World to such a great degree. While it took thousands of years for sugarcane to spread throughout the Old World and products made from it were rare and expensive, that quickly changed when Christopher Columbus loaded cuttings onto his ships for his second voyage to the Americas.[1] Sugarcane was then grown in conquered places using primarily slave or otherwise unfree labor. The resulting products like rum were used to finance larger crops of sugarcane, the purchasing of more slaves, and the conquering of new places. In this chapter, we will begin with an overview of the history of sugar, focusing primarily on the introduction of sugar to the Americas, comparing production across sites during the sixteenth through eighteenth centuries in Barbados, Haiti, the Dominican Republic, Jamaica, Trinidad after slave abolition, Cuba, contemporary Brazil, the United States (specifically Louisiana and Hawai'i), as well as our study area of the Yucatán Peninsula. Lastly, we look at the sugarcane and rum industries in the nineteenth century following the abolition of slavery, noting in particular how plantation and hacienda owners continued to work the labor system to their advantage.

## ORIGINS OF THE SUGAR TRADE

Although commodities such as bananas have a dark history tied to political upheaval and dangerous working conditions, sugarcane production may have been the source of more pain than any other commodity humans have produced.[2] It is important, however, to separate the early cultivation of sugarcane from the exploitative production of something we would recognize as refined sugar today. Peoples of New Guinea were the first to cultivate sugarcane to chew on and extract its juice prior to 8000 BCE, and with the spread of human populations, it reached India by 6000 BCE.[3] Indians first used it as a sweetener and for making non-distilled alcoholic drinks. By the second century CE, the Chinese were cultivating sugarcane, and Saracens (Muslims) introduced sugarcane to Egypt in the seventh century CE.[4] In Europe, sugarcane was cultivated in Madeira (an autonomous region of Portugal), Spain, Cyprus, and Italy by the third century CE, and probably reintroduced into the Iberian Peninsula during the Reconquista conquest period (718 or 720 to 1492 CE).[5] It was likely the Indians who discovered techniques to produce sugar crystals around two thousand years ago, but unmistakable evidence for this is not found until around 500 CE.[6] This was a significant advancement because in this crystalline form, sugar could be made purer, allowing for better preservation.[7]

Polynesian inhabitants in canoes brought sugarcane from the Marquesas to the Hawaiian Islands by 1000 CE.[8] Hawaiians propagated more than twenty named varieties of cane with varying properties and uses. Although they didn't produce refined sugar, they ate the cane during times of famine, used the juice as a food sweetener, added it to medicine, and even added it as an ingredient in love potions. They used the leaves as a wall covering, mulched the tassels, burned the cane stalks to produce dye, and carved the stalks to make spears. They also recognized that standing cane stalks functioned as an effective windbreak along the shoreline.[9]

By 1150 CE, Moorish planters on the southern Iberian Peninsula were growing up to seventy-five thousand acres of sugarcane.[10] After the expulsion of the Moors in 1492, Spain sought new trade routes and sponsored the first of Christopher Columbus's voyages. Soon colonists across the Americas transported rum to Africa and traded it for slaves, and thus were treating humans as commodities.[11] When taken to the Americas, slaves were forced to produce the very products that were used to enslave others.[12] As Foss states, "Rum also fueled what came to be known as the Triangle Trade, in which molasses was exported to New England to be made into rum; rum to Africa to trade for slaves; and slaves to the Caribbean and South America to produce sugar for molasses."[13]

## SUGAR AND THE "AGE OF DISCOVERY" (1500–1800 CE)

Europe's widespread introduction to sugar occurred during the so-called Age of Discovery. Europeans produced sugarcane in Italy, Cyprus, Madeira, and Spain to manufacture products that were medicinal, very expensive, and bore little resemblance to today's refined sugar.[14] Although gold had been the driving force for New World exploration, the reality of its rarity began to take hold and colonizers looked for other commodities to exploit. In 1516, the inspector of gold mines in Hispaniola (now Haiti and the Dominican Republic) presented Spain's King Charles V with sugar loaves as one such option.[15] The desire for sugar and its by-products quickly spread across Europe, and mineral mining was slowly replaced by sugar plantations in the warmer climes of the colonies.[16] While the sugar by-product of rum[17] was produced in countries as distant as England, the United States (in New England), India,[18] South Africa, and Australia, most production was centered in the Caribbean, Central America, and South America.[19]

## SUGARCANE IN THE AMERICAS (1600s–1700s)

Europeans absolutely prized sugar by the late fifteenth century, prompting Columbus to bring sugarcane plants with him on his second voyage to the New World in 1493, with the intent to introduce it to the Americas and export the sugar back home.[20] The Spanish were the first in a line of colonizers on the island of Hispaniola, which was made up of Saint-Domingue (now Haiti) and Santo Domingo (now the Dominican Republic). Spain ceded the western three-eighths of Hispaniola to France in 1502, but built the first sugar mill in the New World circa 1515 on Saint-Domingue.[21] Before 1671, Saint-Domingue had a mixed export economy, with sugar comprising two-thirds of the market, and coffee, indigo, and cotton making up the other third.[22] Sugar plantations in the northern area benefited from rich soil, adequate rainfall, and proximity to the island's political capital, Cap-Français.[23] Planters in the central region of the island had fertile soil but inadequate rainfall that necessitated the building of extensive irrigation systems. Once this infrastructure was in place, the region became home to some the most productive sugar plantations in the Caribbean.[24] With the institution of slave labor, it also became the most profitable colony in the sugar, molasses, and rum trades in the Caribbean.[25]

Sugar was also at the center of a Portugal-controlled Brazil starting in the 1550s, although when the Portuguese discovered gold in the 1590s, it dominated the colony's economic trade for more than a century and downgraded sugar's importance.[26] Brazilian sugar was further undercut when the Dutch established sugar colonies in the Caribbean in the mid-1600s.[27] However, when the gold-mining economy dipped, planters in the Bahia region of the north and the Rio region in the south led efforts to revitalize the sugar economy by reopening old plantations, establishing new ones, and installing modern equipment like steam-powered cane-grinding machines.[28] This brought great wealth, and while the Portuguese never created an aristocracy in Brazil, the title of mill owner (*senhor de engenho*) conferred similar social status.[29] Although mill owners and sugar planters first looked to the Indigenous population to labor in their sugar-cane fields, they refused, even when they placed them under coercive pressure.[30] Thus the sugar industry became dependent upon imported slaves, and they brought in a steady supply to replace the 5 to 10 percent who died each year, and well as to support industry expansion.[31] Estimates vary, but Lockhart and Schwartz report that Brazil probably received about 2.5 million slaves between 1550 and 1800.[32]

Brazil likely produced the first sugarcane spirit, known as *aguardente* (without the "i"), in industrial quantities. As the start-up costs were low, even the smallest sugar mills had an attached distillery, and there were independent distilleries located on many estates.[33] Brazilian aguardente, known as *cachaça*, was the drink of the masses.[34] Yet the government described cachaça as a public nuisance and only allowed slaves to drink it legally.[35]

In Yucatán in southern México, Indigenous Maya had been producing and drinking ritual alcohol for centuries, although sugar-based rum was a new product to the region. The first recorded attempt to grow sugarcane in Yucatán was by the conquistador Francisco de Montejo in the 1530s, when he established a sugar plantation near Champotón in Campeche.[36] However, the Spanish courts stripped Montejo and his family of their labor grants, or encomiendas, after findings surfaced of nepotism and arbitrariness in his exercise of power, causing the venture to fail.[37] Labor shortages limited sugar production until late in the colonial period (mid-sixteenth century to late eighteenth century), and there was a royal prohibition against cane alcohol production until 1796.[38] Historian Robert Patch argues that there was, nonetheless, some cane alcohol produced illegally.[39] Further, based on import records from the 1750s and 1780s, sugar and cane alcohol accounted for approximately 40 percent of the goods imported into Yucatán from other sugar colonies in the Americas.[40]

Colonization first came to the island of Barbados when the English arrived in 1627. They found little trace of the original inhabitants, save the bridge for which the capital, Bridgetown, is named.[41] After Great Britain established its colony, outside enemies left Barbados virtually untouched. It became the first port of call for slave ships, allowing for profitable trade with the Spanish Main and other islands.[42] The island was one of few that did not bounce between European empires, although this did not result in a peaceful existence.[43] As sugar took root as the island's primary export, this increased the need for new lands and more forced laborers. A large number of white farmers were living on the island and growing a variety of fruits and vegetables on small plots of land. However, the sugar growers wanted this land, and they had the economic and political power to get it. Between the years of 1645 to 1667, the number of landed proprietors dropped from 11,200 to 745 as land was consolidated into larger swaths.[44] Scholars believe that most of these small farmers emigrated to other island colonies of Great Britain, where they received the right to partial self-government and freedom from taxation without representation.[45] In return, they were expected to pledge loyalty to the British Parliament.[46] With the decline of the white population, Barbadian planters imported more slaves, increasing the Black population.[47] Between 1645 and 1667, the number of whites decreased from 18,300 down to 8,300, while between 1629 and 1666 the number of enslaved Africans grew from 50 to nearly 60,000 people.[48]

As was the case elsewhere in the Americas, rum production on Barbados was integrated into the industrial portion of the sugar plantation.[49]

Molasses was once a waste product of the sugar-refining process that was dumped or fed to cattle but was now a profitable base ingredient for rum. From the growers' perspective, the geography of Barbados could also be used to their advantage. As the only coral island in the Antilles, the limestone parent material filtered the groundwater and they could easily cultivate its low-lying ground. Further, unlike the mountainous terrain of Jamaica, where slaves often escaped and found refuge, the flat landscape made it easier to control the slave population.[50]

The Spanish had controlled the island of Jamaica since they took it from the Taino Indians in 1494, building two small sugar works during their occupation. In 1655, British forces relocated the two small Spanish sugar works and soon set out to expand production.[51] By 1660, the British wrested the territory away and pacified it by 1664, which was when the true history of Jamaican rum began.[52] The British government appointed Sir Thomas Modyford, a sugar producer and slaveholder from Barbados, as governor of their new colony.[53] Jamaica was an appealing prospect for British settlers because there were also industries tied to cattle, log-wood, and smuggling.[54] By 1665, a large number of English settlers were cultivating cacao and sugarcane, using enslaved Africans brought from Barbados.[55]

Jamaican sugar operations produced three products—molasses, rum, and raw sugar—as mercantile laws precluded them from further refining it into white sugar. As was true elsewhere, the sugar juice found in cut cane decayed rapidly and had to be processed within a few days.[56] Hence each plantation estate was a farm, factory, and rum distillery, with the distillation equipment incorporated into the industrial yard with the rest of the machinery.[57] There were 769 distilleries in 1791 and more than 1,000 just a few years later.[58] To support this dramatic growth, enslaved labor was the economic engine of the island, acting as domestic servants, field laborers, artisans, and small-scale traders. Jamaica quickly became the British Caribbean's leading sugar colony and remained so throughout the slave period.[59] As plantations grew, so did the ratio of Black slaves to whites, by at least ten to one in 1775.[60] The importation of enslaved Africans throughout the slave period permanently changed the ethnic makeup of the island, which today is more than 90 percent Black.[61]

Compared to Barbados and Jamaica, Cuba came relatively late to the sugar trade. Starting around 1715, the Spanish took over many munic-ipalities to control smuggling, and local governments, or cabildos, lost their ability to give unused agricultural lands to local residents.[62] The Spanish state further hampered economic growth in Cuba by imposing state-sponsored monopolies on commerce. For instance, in 1717 all tobacco production was placed under a royal monopoly known as the Factoriá de Tobacos. In 1740, the Royal Company of Commerce (Real Compañia de Comercio) received a monopoly on trade between Cuba and Spain. Spaniards could buy Cuban goods at low prices, while Spanish goods were sold on the island at high markups. This continued to slow the Cuban economy and often resulted in food shortages in Havana.[63] However, during an eleven-month period in which Britain controlled Cuba (1762–63), they imported ten thousand slaves, and shipping traffic increased from low double digits per year to more than ten thousand ships.[64] This was the catalyst needed for Cuba's sugar industry, and the economy flourished with the removal of trade barriers between Cuba and Spain.

In the United States it was taxation that complicated sugar and rum production. In the seventeenth century, New England producers relied primarily on French molasses, as it was generally available at lower prices. This was because French rum production used sugarcane juice exclusively, and they dumped their molasses on the market, as they had no other use for it.[65] However, the Molasses Act of 1733 designated the British Caribbean sugar producers as their only legal suppliers and taxed all non-British molasses, effectively doubling the price of French molasses. The intent of the act was to benefit the Caribbean planters while harming New Englanders, as Britain viewed their financial success as a threat. However, under a lax enforcement system, the duty was rarely paid, and those caught smuggling encountered bribable officials.[66] The Molasses Act was then replaced by the Sugar Act of 1764, which lowered the tax rate to three pence per gallon of molasses. This act included better enforcement mechanisms and stiff penalties for evading it, including for smuggling molasses produced outside the British Empire. U.S. rum producers protested that any tax on rum production was too great, as their profit margins were already too narrow. While a gallon of molasses could produce a gallon of rum, it was only affordable to produce when molasses was cheap.[67]

However, French colonists were instrumental in introducing sugarcane in Louisiana, when in 1751 they imported cane varieties from Santo Domingo.[68] Planter Joseph Solis founded a sugarcane mill around 1784 that focused on producing small quantities of crystalline sugar and tafia rum, which is generally considered a lower quality rum made from impure molasses. The fledgling industry ended when the colony passed into Spanish hands in 1763, although interest in sugar production was revived in the 1790s.[69] Starting in 1808, tafia production increased with the improvement of the sugar industry infrastructure, and by 1810 seventeen distilleries were in operation.[70]

Although Hawaiians had been growing sugarcane since Polynesians introduced it around 1000 CE, they did not refine sugar or distill rum. It wasn't until Captain James Cook and the British claimed the islands in 1778 that they began importing sugarcane-based rum.[71] The famed King Kamehameha liked rum so much that he ordered it to be produced locally, although other island rulers tried to ban its importation after seeing its effect on British sailors.[72]

Meanwhile, Haiti's sugar industry was propelled by France's insatiable sugar consumption, requiring the colonists to import half a million slaves by 1789.[73] Under the horrible working conditions of French colonialism, enslaved workers led the Haitian Revolution, which lasted from 1791–1804 and destroyed many of the sugar plantations. This ultimately led to the abolition of slavery and the establishment of the Independent Empire of Haiti.[74] This collapse of the Haitian sugar market benefited Spanish-run Cuba, as they became the main source of sugar for the United States after 1791.[75] Although by 1850 Cuba was the top cane producer in the world, Spanish troops worked closely with wealthy sugar planters to maintain their control of the large slave population, as they feared a revolt similar to that in Haiti.[76]

## THE NINETEENTH CENTURY: SUGARCANE AND RUM FOLLOWING REBELLION AND ABOLITION

After the abolition of slavery in Haiti and other Caribbean nations, emancipation took many years to transition to free wage labor and, in many ways, conditions stayed virtually the same.[77] For example, before slavery was finally abolished in the British Caribbean in 1838, there was a transitional term of "apprenticeship" that extended slavery for up to eight years for most slaves.[78] Plantation owners fought abolition because of the expected high costs of paying workers, but this was based on paying all the slaves the top pay rate. In reality, the costs of paying wages were lower than the costs to feed, house, and provide medical care for slaves.[79] Politics also remained volatile following abolition and independence. Countries like Haiti paid a steep price for their violent break with slavery and colonialism. France imposed sharp costs in exchange for recognizing Haiti's independence, which greatly hampered its development.[80] Independence was also a shaky transition. Santo Domingo (part of Hispaniola) declared its independence from Spain in 1821, only to be conquered by Haiti the next year. Then Haitians were expelled from Santo Domingo in 1844, when it was declared an independent Dominican Republic.[81]

Labor conditions in the Dominican Republic took a different trajectory compared with those of other Caribbean countries. In most of the Caribbean, as slavery and other coercive labor systems weakened over time, the civil rights of workers grew, ultimately transitioning to free labor.[82] Instead, in the Dominican Republic, free labor gave way over time to a system in which the government oversaw a labor organization that was semicoerced.[83] Elsewhere, planters used similar tactics to ensure that workers had few, if any, alternatives to working on plantations after abolition.[84]

In Louisiana, the nineteenth century was a difficult era for the sugar industry. Most planters opposed secession prior to the Civil War, despite wanting the institution of slavery to continue. During the war, the sugar industry was greatly impacted when much of their processing equipment was damaged.[85] Further, when federal troops arrived in Louisiana, they raised the hopes of the slave population, who refused to work even though the war was not yet over.[86] After the war, growers faced a labor shortage, as the Black population had been diminished by emigration and death, and women and children often refused to work in the fields. They also had trouble securing loans to repair their equipment, causing the 1865 harvest to be the smallest on record.[87]

This gave laborers leverage, and in December of 1865, the Freedmen's Bureau set new employment conditions, which included twenty-six working days a month, after which additional compensation was due; freedom to choose an employer; and benefits, including food, clothing, medical care, and schooling for children.[88] The resulting work contracts, often between freed slaves and their former masters, usually included possible shares of the profits at the end of the year.[89] While the perishable nature of sugarcane continued to create intense work schedules for laborers during the harvest season, planters were now dealing with freedmen and freedwomen. Workers were well aware of their ability to disrupt the operation of the plantations or strike when treated poorly. The collective power of workers grew as labor shortages drove wages up until the price of sugar crashed in 1873.[90] Despite these improvements, former slaves worked as gang labor, lived in former slave housing, and were still under the direction of white overseers.

In Brazil in the late 1820s and early 1830s, planters and merchants were focused on a modernization agenda, facilitated by the formation of the Sociedade Auxiliadora da Indústria Nacional (SAIN) and the Sociedade de Agricultura, Comercio e Industria (SACI).[91] These efforts benefited affluent areas like Bahia that had modern and more efficient steam-driven mills, and left behind poorer areas like Pernambuco that lacked modern technology.[92] Brazil's sugar economy continued to modernize through the early mid-nineteenth century but politics led it into decline. European sugar importers favored their own colonial holdings, shunning independent Brazil.[93] Brazil was further disadvantaged when the international slave trade ended in 1850, causing labor shortages and an increase in the price for any slave that was traded within the country.[94] Some Europeans used Brazil's continued status as slaveholders as yet another reason to refuse to do business with them.[95]

By the late 1870s in Brazil, the sugar industry was reorganized from a model of family-run plantations to one of agribusiness. This meant that boards of directors ran the large companies and their performance could be judged from the outside. Small plantations were also impacted by an 1881 law that stated slaves could be used on the agricultural side of the industry, but that only freemen could work in the sugar refineries. As the small plantations could not compete with refineries under this law, many abandoned refining and shifted their efforts toward rum production.[96] Other planters also produced more cane to meet the increased capacity of the larger refineries. This attracted foreign capital, and soon the Dutch, British, and French upgraded equipment in regions with less-advanced technology. The refining industry came to be dominated by foreign ownership in some regions, even though they paid low prices for cane and were selective about which farmers they would work with.[97]

Brazil continued to face challenges after 1884 as crop prices dropped due to increased sugar-beet production in Europe.[98] Further, the mills in northeastern Brazil were limited in size due to topographic and soil challenges. Competing Cuban factories dwarfed those of Brazil and touted better technology.[99] Yet Brazilian sugar remained competitive due to local exploitative labor practices and environmental advantages. Companies paid wages that were one-fourth of those in Cuba, and Cuba's advanced technology was negated by Brazil's availability of water-power.[100] However, slaves became increasingly emboldened to refuse to work or simply fled, affecting planters and the refiners who had no cane to process. Brazil finally abolished slavery in 1888, although, like elsewhere, it was replaced with new forms of exploitation under tenancy.[101]

In Barbados at the end of the 1800s, the sugar and rum industries shrank dramatically under the inefficiencies of slavery, although following abolition, plantation owners ran hobbled sugar factories and rum distilleries for another hundred years.[102] In 1906, to placate merchants who feared independent distillers were going to erode their monopoly, the government of Barbados passed a law stating the producer could only sell their rum in quantities of ten gallons or more. This meant that producers could not bottle or market their own rum for individual sale.[103]

Jamaican producers, who were known for producing harsh, dark rums with a high alcohol content, continued to expand and innovate their mills. In the 1820s steam power replaced wind, water, and animal power.[104] Production became centralized in fewer and fewer companies, and the stills became larger.[105] However, after 1838, labor shortages inevitably led to a decline in sugar production and, with it, the economy of Jamaica. Attempting to cope, planters imported laborers from India after former slaves refused or were barred from doing free labor.[106] As the labor drop-off continued, estates that once oppressed native inhabitants and drove the island economy were abandoned and left to waste away.[107]

On the island of St. Croix following the end of slavery, plantation owners worked the system to their advantage by developing yearlong labor contracts that once accepted by a laborer could not be broken. The contract renewed automatically unless individual workers notified managers that they wanted to dissolve the relationship, which could only be done at set times of the year.[108] When former slaves resisted the contract system by refusing to work unless the contract lengths were shortened, some plantation owners evicted workers from their homes. Similarly, once workers left the plantation, farm owners sometimes had them arrested for trespassing when they visited family members still living there.[109] Out of desperation, some former slaves squatted on lands that they held no legal right to; others resorted to sharecropping.[110] However, this was done on the most marginal land, so the former slaves took all the risk and the landowner shared in any rewards.[111]

In Louisiana after abolition, planters tried to continue to dominate in the lives of their Black employees, including their political affiliations, by harassing or discharging members of the Republican Party.[112] Politically active workers helped organize resistance against gang labor throughout the South, which resulted in access to land for both tenancy and sharecropping. It also decentralized settlement, hampering their ability for collective self-defense and other action.[113] Planters realized that with Black participation in politics and voting, they would not regain control of their former slaves.[114] Planters attempted to counter the growth of the Republican Party on the plantations by demanding certificates prior to hiring that were granted to those who pledged to vote for Democratic Party candidates.[115] When such measures failed, planters and conservative allies used violence and threats of violence to keep Black voters away from the polls. This demonstrated that federal involvement was needed to ensure Blacks had access to the political process and resulted in planters turning to immigrant labor.[116]

By 1870, foreigners, especially Italians, made up much of the labor force in Louisiana during the cane harvest.[117] While there, foreigners were paid at the rate given to Black laborers, helping but not solving the labor-shortage problem.[118] Perhaps as a result of class solidarity, all workers at the plantation—Black, Italian, and French—worked well together without hostility.[119] Italian laborers were sometimes able to save enough from their meager earnings to move out of the free-labor pool to sharecrop or even own their own land.[120] However, the social climate of Louisiana tolerated the lynching of Italians. That, along with better-paying jobs in construction, caused Italians to leave agricultural labor and, in some cases, Louisiana altogether.[121]

In Hawaiʻi, the government instituted the Masters and Servants Act of 1850, modeled after the United States Seaman Shipping Act. The act recognized two types of servants: apprentices learning to become skilled laborers and those who earned wages.[122] It was intended to tie workers to plantations for fixed terms of service while also protecting them from some form of abuse. For instance, the act allowed the docking of wages for missed work, but not nonproductive or inefficient labor.[123] Rules published in 1866 by the Bureau of Immigration further codified the docking of a quarter-day's wages for fifteen minutes of tardiness and two days for an absence of one day.[124]

Overseers could also propose a "stint" project to be completed that day, allowing laborers to choose between accepting the stint or working the normal ten-hour day.[125] While possibly appealing, a stint could conceivably be used to increase the expectations of how much work was possible per day, potentially affecting the amount of normal work expected during normal shifts. Despite prohibitions on the practice, some plantations fined workers or whipped workers for slow work, insubordination, or drunkenness.[126] Revisions to the constitution in 1852 included prohibitions in involuntary service.[127] Over the next decades, the Hawaiian government tightened the laws and practices to exert more control over the lives of workers, including acquitting fewer workers accused of deserting service through time.[128]

The growing cycle of sugarcane is long in Hawai'i—normally lasting between eighteen to twenty-four months and up to thirty-six months in some areas of higher elevation.[129] Despite their long experience in growing cane, Hawaiians were unskilled in producing sugar and were usually unwilling to stay on the plantations for an entire average two-year growing cycle, reducing growers' yields. While the Hawaiian sugar industry imported labor from Africa, many more workers came from China, Japan, Korea, and the Philippines. Like planters in other countries, they paid workers in scrip or in kind, tying the worker to the company store and making it difficult to seek employment elsewhere.[130]

The planter's cartel founded the Hawaiian Sugar Producers Association (HSPA) in 1894 to further advance their interests.[131] From 1896 to 1932, as production quadrupled and labor doubled (from twenty-five thousand to fifty thousand), the number of plantations declined. As the "Big Five" growers edged out smaller and weaker companies, they dropped from fifty-six to forty-six plantations.[132] Hawaiian growers also experimented with giving a group of laborers land and materials to produce cane for a predetermined price, and attempted to address the problem of absenteeism.[133] The HSPA established a bonus system that (1) was payable when those who earned less than twenty-four dollars per month completed twenty days of work and (2) paid 1 percent of annual earnings for every dollar over seventy dollars that a ton of sugar traded for at wholesale.[134] Striking workers and management adjusted the bonus amount, requirements, and payment cycle multiple times.[135] Planters responded by ensuring the passage of legislation that made it easier to hamper union activity and harass striking workers.[136]

The connections between sugar labor and rum in Hawai'i are not nearly as clear as they are in other sugar-producing areas, and prohibition had been in place since 1840. While the habitual use of alcohol was sparked by colonialism, it was early missionaries that tried to stamp it out, even when rum was considered a normal part of a sugar plantation.[137] In 1826, John Wilkinson, a man with experience on plantations in the British West Indies, started a sugar mill and rum distillery on the island of Oahu. Upon Wilkinson's death, Boki, the governor of Oahu, gained control over the operation but failed to produce significant quantities of sugar or rum during his first season, despite employing more than one hundred laborers. One plausible explanation of Boki's initial failure is that the intensity of labor needed to operate a profitable sugar plantation was incompatible with what a Hawaiian leader could extract from his worker-subjects. Boki then partnered with *haole* (non-Indigenous) investors from Honolulu, throwing an "intemperate" celebration that drew the ire of missionaries working in the area. The missionaries, aided by one of Boki's political rivals, eventually caused his operation to fail.[138]

During the first annual meeting of the Royal Hawaiian Agricultural Society, a resolution in support of repeal of the 1840 law prohibiting manufacture of rum was introduced. The repeal proponents offered to provide "aid [to planters] in carrying on their plantations" as a rationale for repeal. The resolution failed.[139] While the meaning of "aid" is ambiguous, it may have included provisioning workers with liquor. Despite being outlawed, Japanese workers in particular engaged in the illicit manufacturing and sale of alcohol, including distilled spirits.[140] Ultimately, prohibition was repealed in 1874. This may have been because as the Hawaiian sugar industry consolidated, only the largest planters could operate on a profit if unable to turn their waste products into rum.[141]

What this brief comparative history shows is that across the Americas following the end of slavery, many plantation owners imposed economic conditions on former slaves that were comparable to those they experienced under servitude. In the next chapter, we shift our focus to the particular production methods and coercive labor system planters employed in the Americas to produce sugar and rum from sugarcane.

# CHAPTER 2

# COERCED LABOR AND SUGAR ACROSS THE AMERICAS

IN THIS CHAPTER, WE WILL compare and contrast the sugar planta-tions and rum distilleries across the Americas in the nineteenth century, and then specifically compare them with that of the sugar haciendas and rum distilleries of the Yucatán Peninsula during the same time period. In this discussion we will examine the details of the labor systems used, the sugar production and rum distillation processes, and the living conditions of the laborers, including immigrants. Throughout this chapter we will argue that although the scales of production vary and there are some clear regional distinctions in terms of labor practices, the owners and growers consistently used the labor system to their advantage, while the laborers found ways to actively resist these forced conditions.

## COERCED LABOR SYSTEMS

We want to begin by defining indentured servitude, debt peonage,[1] and chattel slavery,[2] which are coercive labor systems that secured workers to perform labor on an ongoing basis that few wanted to do. Chattel slavery is the concept that humans can be owned, traded, or inherited. While indentured service and debt peonage are not slavery, the distinc-tions between them vary with the level of restriction of peons across time and place.[3] Indentured servitude is the exchange of a predetermined period of unpaid labor, most often five years, usually in exchange for the cost of passage to a new place.[4] In the Caribbean, many of the first unfree laborers in the Caribbean were indentured servants.[5] This included some Europeans who were fleeing poverty in their home countries.[6] In places like the Yucatán Peninsula under debt peonage, laborers accepted loans from hacienda owners (or owners of other business[7]) that both parties knew were unlikely to ever be fully repaid.[8] As the debt peon became more indebted, their legal rights of free movement became more restricted. Deeply indebted peons needed permission from the hacienda owner or their agent to leave the property. Peons would be free upon repayment of the debt owed, but inability to ever repay loans made peonage effectively permanent for most.[9] In contrast, for those of African descent brought to Barbados to support a fast-growing sugar industry, the British adopted the system of chattel slavery, which had no basis in law.[10] While European indentured servants were freed at the end of a term of service, Africans became the permanent property of their owners, and this status also passed to their children.[11] The Barbadian slave code was then copied and/or emulated in Antigua, Jamaica, South Carolina, and Virginia.[12]

In Brazil, the Portuguese system differed from the British, French, and American forms of chattel slavery in at least one key way. Manumission (the act of an owner freeing his or her slaves) was a central component of slave systems based in Iberian traditions. Slaves owners in Brazil were much more likely to free their slaves, either during their lifetime or in their wills. Women were more likely to be freed, possibly due to the incidences of fraternization between owners and slave women. Trusted slaves, mulatto children of the owner, and others were sometimes freed by their master, while others bought their own freedom or were freed after purchase by their family.[13]

Some portion of the workforce in places with chattel slavery was composed of free laborers and indentured servants, and the workforce in places with debt peonage also included free laborers. In both cases, owners viewed slaves and debt peons as a long-term investment, while free laborers and the indentured could be worked to the point of exhaustion or chronic illness and then replaced. Plantation owners had a limited term in which to extract their investment from indentured servants, even if overwork caused health problems later after their period of indenture had ended.[14]

## SUGARCANE CULTIVATION

Although the amount of land dedicated to growing sugarcane varied widely by region, cultivation methods were virtually the same everywhere. Workers generally propagated new sugarcane from the cuttings taken from the top of mature stalks of cane. The stalks were similar in appearance to bamboo (a relative of sugarcane) and generally stood a foot to a foot and a half tall. They contained two to three joints, along which the new stalks would grow.[15] Generally, the farther sugarcane was cultivated from the equator, the longer it would take to grow to maturation.[16] Freezes could heavily damage crops, as sugarcane is not freeze tolerant, and a frost could make it harder to extract the juice. Sugarcane was thus best suited to tropical and subtropical environments, particularly hot, humid environments with high rainfall. Cane grew best in climates with 1.8 to 2.5 meters of rain per year, but new stalks could be damaged by overwatering.[17]

Laborers across the Americas prepared their fields by digging furrows (long, narrow trenches) and planting the cuttings horizontally. If cuttings were planted upright, the new stalks would not grow. Weeding was important during cane maturation to reduce competition with other plants and to control pest populations. Workers everywhere harvested sugarcane by cutting the stalks near but above ground level with hook-shaped knives or machetes.[18] By leaving a small piece of the stalk and the intact roots, this perennial continued to produce.[19] Harvesters had to carefully navigate around the sugarcane leaves to avoid being cut by their sharp edges. Sometimes they would burn the sugarcane fields at harvesttime to reduce the amount of unusable plant material such as leaves, while also killing off microorganisms and aiding in soil fertility.[20] While the burning did kill the remaining stalk, it did not generally damage the root structure. Once burned, they had to harvest the field immediately or the cane would begin to decay. While the fires sped up the harvesting process, it could place a grower in a vulnerable position if there were accidental fires or there were too few workers available to process the cut cane. As the workers knew this, the act of burning fields near harvesttime sometimes became an effective mode of resistance.[21] Once harvested, laborers "dressed" the cane by stripping the stalks of any remaining leaves, stacking or bundling them, and shipping them to the mill for processing.[22]

**FIGURE I.** Xuxub sugar-refining building, with a diagram of a Jamaica Train. (Photograph by Jennifer P. Mathews; diagram from Olcott 1857, 94.)

## THE SUGAR- AND RUM-MAKING PROCESSES

Workers had to send stalks to the grinding mill and extract the juice soon after cutting, as the sugars would break down quickly.[23] The first mills in the Americas were powered by animal or human traction. However, as technology and infrastructure improved, larger plantations introduced steam, gas, and then electrically powered mills.[24] As workers extracted the cane juice, they would then pump or pour it into large metal vats to cook it down. The juice was usually quite dirty, so workers added slaked lime to clarify and clean it during cooking.[25]

The earliest sugarhouse design was known as the "Spanish Train," which used individual heat sources under each kettle.[26] This evolved into to the "Jamaica Train" design, which had a string of large kettles that lay in between a single heat source and the smokestack.[27] One benefit of the Jamaica Train (figure 1) over the Spanish Train was its fuel efficiency. Spanish Trains required mass quantities of firewood that burned very hot, while Jamaica Trains retained more heat and could use the crushed cane stalks, known as *bagasse*.[28] As workers boiled the water in the cane juice off, they moved the increasingly sugary syrup from kettle to kettle to control its temperature. At any point during the concentration process, workers could add more slaked lime to further clarify the syrup.[29]

Once boiled down, the worker cooled down the cane syrup and added sugar crystals to seed crystal development. At this point the process could vary along two trajectories. The older, simpler, and more labor-intensive process was known as *claying*. This involved placing crystalized sugar in conical, semiporous ceramic pots, and slowly running water through the pot to wash away the molasses, eventually resulting in white (or whitened) sugar.[30] This was typical on smaller plantations across the Americas and at haciendas in Yucatán. The newer and more complex process (typical of larger plantations in places like Brazil and Cuba) used centrifuges to separate the molasses from the sugar through centrifugal force, resulting in purer sugar. Sugarhouse workers placed the crystalline sugar in the centrifuges and added water to make the molasses thinner. The centrifuges spun the molasses solution away from the sugar, and once stopped, the worker could remove the watery molasses repeatedly until the sugar reached the desired purity.

Many Caribbean colonies shipped unrefined sugar to Europe to avoid the extra duties on semirefined sugar imposed by the colonial powers (see chapter 1). In this case, workers interrupted the process immediately after the sugar crystals had formed. Workers then packed the sugar into hogshead barrels (a large cask for storing food commodities or liquids) and waited twelve to fourteen hours before draining and collecting the molasses that had settled to the bottom.[31] This interruption of the refining process did not seem to affect the quality of the final product.

Makers across the Americas used varying amounts of molasses in rum production, ranging from using none at all to deriving rum entirely from molasses.[32] Most rum was (and is) made from molasses collected during the boiling, refining, and packing processes.[33] Using molasses for making rum adds to the value of the sugarcane crop by using something that would otherwise be discarded as waste or fed to animals.[34] In French-controlled territories, distillers used cane syrup without removing any molasses to produce *rhum agricole*. This meant there was no need to boil the cane juice down to a crystalline state.[35] However, in most other locations, a distiller would place the sugar and molasses in a fermentation tank and pour water in to achieve the desired ratio of water to sugar. The sugary water would then begin to ferment because of yeasts naturally present in the environment, although most contemporary distillers add yeast collected from previous successful batches.[36] In particular, adding yeast of known strains speeds up fermentation and makes results more predictable.[37]

Predictability in production during the nineteenth century would have been particularly challenging. Once the fermentation process had begun, making rum in small batches was more art than science. With experience the distiller learned when fermentation had completed, based on the look and the taste of the resultant alcohol-laden liquid.[38] Once fermented, the distiller pumped or poured the liquid into the still and heated it to evaporate the alcohol. As alcohol has a lower boiling temperature than water, this separated most of it from the water.[39]

During the nineteenth and into the early twentieth century, most rum distilleries in the Caribbean and Yucatán used simple pot stills to produce rum in small batches.[40] The first and last portions of the distillation run were known as the "heads" and "tails," respectively, and were poisonous. The distiller knew by taste when the heads had been boiled off and began collecting the rum that ran out of the still. Eventually the taste of the rum changed again, indicating that the usable portion of the distillation run had ended. Heads were mostly usable alcohol and, if retained, the distiller could add them back into to the still during the next distillation run.[41] The tails were not usable for consumptive purposes. The rum could vary quite a bit from batch to batch, and distillers could add water to dilute the rum to the preferred alcohol content. The storage conditions and whether the rum was aged greatly affected the taste and appearance of the end product. Today, continuous-column stills remove much of the head and tail fractions, making mass-produced rum much more consistent in taste.[42] Most rum aficionados today prefer high-quality small-batch rums to drink straight, which would be similar in scale to what distillers were making on nineteenth-century plantations and haciendas.

While the range of rum productions methods and equipment was similar in the Caribbean and the Yucatán Peninsula, the social relations at sugar and rum-making operations differed greatly. This was due to regional differences in the capitalization of productions sites and in the ways that owners were able to coerce laborers into working at the operation.

## SUGARCANE PLANTATIONS VERSUS SUGARCANE HACIENDAS

To this point, we have primarily discussed sugar plantations, which were agricultural estates found across the Americas that were run by dominant owners organized into a corporation. Backed by abundant capital, they oversaw a dependent labor force to supply a large-scale market. The goal was to further the accumulation of capital without reference to the status needs of the owners. In contrast, the nineteenth-century factory farms in the Yucatán Peninsula better conform to Wolf and Mintz's description of "haciendas." These were agricultural estates with a dominant landowner that oversaw a dependent labor force and supplied a small-scale market with limited capital. Using the means of production, they accumulated more capital to reinvest into the infrastructure and to support the aspirations of the owner.[43]

There are two caveats to these definitions. First, these institutions differed along a continuum rather than as binaries, as plantations and haciendas could vary in size and complexity, and owners from both were known to show off their wealth. Second, these designations differ regionally. A factory farm in Yucatán that fit all the criteria of a *plantation* would still be called an *hacienda*, just as a farm in the southern U.S. that met the definition of *hacienda* would still be referred to as a *plantation*. Haciendas in Yucatán (in and around Mérida)[44] that produced henequen[45] were generally landholdings that included masonry boundary walls, fields for growing the crop or crops, processing equipment, and a main house for the owner or property manager.[46] Haciendas in the eastern Yucatán Peninsula fit the social criteria as laid out by Wolf and Mintz, but lack much of this infrastructure. For example, the historic sugar-producing operations we have investigated in the Yalahau region in the northeast corner of the Yucatán Peninsula (figure 3) lack the typical boundary walls, and the main houses were reportedly more modest than most. Thus, although our sites are atypical of the physical form known for henequen, we refer to them as *haciendas* because they fit this designation based on the relations of production.

For the owners, sugar haciendas in nineteenth-century Yucatán were immensely profitable. The return on investment was up to 700 percent, and initial start-up costs could be recouped by the second year.[47] However, like the less-profitable henequen haciendas, the wages for the workers were extremely low and were sometimes paid in the form of rum or, more often, company scrip, instead of cash.[48] We believe that managers offered comparable wages to those offered by less-profitable haciendas to ensure a dependent and pliant workforce and to increase their profits. Payment in scrip only usable at the company store reinforced this cycle of dependency and kept all profits in house, as workers used scrip to purchase meager rations, clothing, and tools. It was easy for a family to

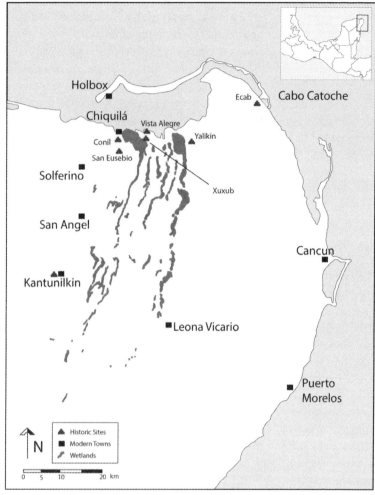

**MAP 2.** The Yalahau region. (Adapted from map courtesy of Jeffrey B. Glover.)

become more indebted because they had to purchase the basic necessities of life from this monopolistic source.[49]

Unlike the steady workforce needed for henequen, the work schedule on sugar haciendas was uneven. There were times of the year when the sugar haciendas needed little to no labor, while at other times, the work continued around the clock. Particularly during harvesttime, workers had to put in long hours to process the cane immediately. For example, Meyers and Carlson document that sugar workers at Hacienda Tabi in Yucatán worked fourteen- to fifteen-hour shifts, while Wells and Joseph cite an example from Cuba in which slaves were operating grinding mills and moving superheated cane syrup from kettle to kettle for up to twenty hours per day.[50] This work was performed under threat of physical punishment for slow or inferior performance.[51]

Sugar workers experienced greater hardships than hacienda laborers working other cash crops. First, sugar workers were less likely to live on the hacienda grounds than henequen workers.[52] While this provided a bit more separation from the prying eyes of the hacienda managers, it also meant having to provide for their own housing. Second, the sugar-planting and harvest schedule directly conflicted with the traditional farming schedule.[53] From a philosophical position, this is a problem because Maya cultural identity is inextricably linked to subsistence farming.[54] From a more utilitarian perspective, conflict between sugar and subsistence agriculture schedules was a problem because it meant that workers had to purchase staple foods from meager earnings, instead of producing them for themselves. The largely Maya working class had few options.

A significant distinction between sugar haciendas in Yucatán and sugar plantations elsewhere across the Americas is for whom they were producing. In Yucatán they only produced enough sugar and rum to be used as a domestic product, often having to import additional stores from elsewhere in the Caribbean.[55] In contrast, foreign planters on colonial plantations were beholden to produce commodities for the benefit of their home countries. Regulations limited the export of fully finished goods from the colonies to ensure that firms in Europe profited from the colonies as well. For instance, crystalline sugar was shipped to Europe, where it was further processed into products such as rum and refined sugar.[56] With increased availability during the sixteenth century, sugar quickly shifted from being a luxury of the rich to a staple of the poor by the nineteenth century. They added sugar to their otherwise bland diets, further driving up demand. Rum was also distributed throughout Europe, gaining a foothold in countries like Germany that had no significant New World colonial presence.[57]

## WORKING AND LIVING CONDITIONS ON SUGAR PLANTATIONS AND HACIENDAS

In general, within the labor forces of sugar plantations there was an internal class system that benefited those workers with higher status. In fact, the owners and managers usually chose the lowest-level overseer from the ranks of workers for their ability to keep others working, whether they were debt peons or slaves.[58] In the slavery system of the Caribbean and Brazil, owners treated skilled slaves better than indentured servants, as they considered them vital parts of their operation.[59] They could be hired out to generate extra income for the plantation and could work for themselves or their owners on Sunday to make extra money. Skilled slaves were also more likely to buy their own freedom.[60] Slave owners provided housing and issued food and clothing rations to slaves, and in some places in the Caribbean they gave cash or in-kind bonuses at Christmas.[61] For debt peons, the benefits included loans to pay for rites of passage, exemption from taxation and military service, staple foods at below-market rates, and in some cases, housing, food, and clothing rations. Skilled workers in Yucatán also enjoyed better pay and more privileges.[62] Slaves and debt peons usually received medical care, access to land for farming, reduced workload in their old age, and sometimes rum, either as a ration or a reward.[63]

In some regions, native populations fled or refused to work, regardless of coercion by colonial settlers.[64] Their knowledge of the local terrain, its resources, and extended social networks sometimes allowed them to avoid the entrapment into forced labor. In Jamaica, the mountainous landscape allowed slaves to flee, whereas in Barbados, the flatness of the island made it easier to physically control slaves. A notable exception was Mapps Cave, where slaves hid to drink and have a break from their daily lives, and where they planned the 1816 slave rebellion.[65]

Working conditions on sugar plantations in places like Barbados varied dramatically from agricultural systems in Europe or even sugar production in México. Sugar was a year-round pursuit in Barbados, without downtime or off-seasons.[66] The "workweek . . . began at 1 A.M. on Monday and continued around the clock in four-hour shifts until midnight the following Saturday, when religion, at least, forbade such toil."[67] The process was so well tuned that any disruption left everyone standing around as the production halted.[68] The stripping of the trees while clearing land for fields and monocropping led to the loss of soil fertility, which necessitated more expensive and labor-intensive methods, like planting cane in holes and fertilizing with dung.[69] The result was that only the richest families in Barbados could afford sugar plantations, due to the need for a large number of slaves and expensive equipment. As more of the land was concentrated in fewer hands, there was no place for a free white population, as the island was devoted almost totally to sugar production.[70]

In Brazil many mill owners rented land to independent farmers (*lavradores*), collecting 60 percent of the crop in rent. Most lavradores were Portuguese or Brazilian-born whites and included a broad swath of the elite population, including military men, priests, merchants, and widows, although occasionally lower-class people owned a few acres that they worked themselves.[71] Mill owners preferred to rent to farmers with slaves and oxen, as they produced more sugarcane.[72] In a pattern that repeats elsewhere, slavery also impacted the social and economic mobility of the landless working class. Slave labor continued to depress skilled workers' wages and status, despite their attempts to gain seats in government and to gain economic influence.[73]

In many places across the Americas, Indigenous populations were significantly reduced (by as much as 90 percent) due to European-introduced diseases.[74] For example, early descriptions of the colony said that Barbados was disease-ridden and thus a dangerous place to live.[75] Although health conditions improved and disease rates dropped as the colony was established, the island remained dangerous for slaves, due to malnutrition, physical trauma, severe infection, and an overall low life expectancy.[76] Sheridan reports that Barbadian sugar plantation owners had to replace nearly 5 percent of their enslaved workforce each year just to retain the status quo.[77] This was an intense financial drain on the plantation owners, also further illustrating the brutal living conditions of the enslaved population.

## IMMIGRANTS IN THE CANE FIELDS

Near the end of legal slavery and after the slave trade was abolished in the United States and Latin America, planters returned to using immigrant labor. The countries of origin where most of the laborers hailed from shifted. Early labor was attracted from western Europe and Africa, and later eastern Europeans and Asians formed the great majority of imported labor. The exception is the Dominican Republic, which instead attracted and abused the neighboring, primarily Black, Haitian population. The following discussion explores the use of immigrant labor on sugar plantations in Trinidad, the United States (Louisiana and Hawai'i), the Dominican Republic, and Yucatán. Whether permanent emigration from their homelands was their intent or not, many of these workers stayed, married, and had children in the places they ventured to for work. Perhaps not on the scale of the changes caused in the Caribbean by the slave trade, these workers nonetheless permanently changed the culture of their new homes.

In Trinidad, after slavery was abolished, French planters faced labor shortages, and growers began importing East Indian indentured servants. In 1851, the island introduced five-year contracts through which, upon completion followed by five years as a free laborer, the worker would either be repatriated or receive five acres of land.[78] While indentured, servants escaped drudgery through the ritual use of marijuana, and they also sometimes planted cannabis rather than food crops on their land allocations and sold the product at a profit.[79] Planters saw this enterprise as being at cross-purposes with the work of the plantation, as it was fostering a less-dependent workforce.[80] They countered this with claims similar to those made by William Randolph Hearst and *Reefer Madness* in the United States, spreading the idea that cannabis caused violent crime.[81] Planters nonetheless sold marijuana to indentured servants through their company stores, although they ultimately switched to selling rum, as they had monopoly control and could make a greater profit.[82]

In the United States, planters complained that Black laborers were unreliable, inefficient, left for jobs in the city, and did not produce as much as expected.[83] This relationship was further eroded when Black agricultural workers organized strikes—including one that turned violent in St. Bernard Parish in Louisiana in 1881.[84] Planters blamed Black workers for wanting better wages and for failing to meet quotas.[85] This may have been because they were unwilling to continue working like slaves, while the white workers, who had more upward mobility, worked as much as possible, saving to buy land or open businesses.[86] Facing labor shortages after slave emancipation in the United States, sugar-plantation owners began employing foreigners (especially Italians) in the cane fields at harvesttime, easing but not solving their labor problems.[87] While these Italian workers were sometimes able to save enough to sharecrop or even buy some land of their own, threats of lynching drove many out of Louisiana agriculture.[88]

Native Hawaiians, despite growing sugarcane for centuries, were generally unskilled at producing sugar, and few would stay for the entire eighteen-, twenty-four-, or even thirty-six-month growing cycle.[89] The Hawaiian sugar industry imported labor from Africa, but many more workers came from China, Japan, Korea, the Philippines, Russia, and Portugal. Chinese immigrants, followed by small numbers of Portuguese, Russian, and then Japanese immigrants, were contracted as labor first, but planters viewed the Chinese and Japanese workers as less than ideal, as they often left for other work after their contract was over, and there were far too few Portuguese or Russian workers to meet the demand for labor.[90] To take advantage of ethnic differences, managers segregated the living quarters in camps. While the workers preferred it, owners could pit workers of varying ethnicities against each other and pay differential wages by ethnicity instead of productivity or other changeable factors.[91] Ultimately, Hawaiian planters relied on Filipino laborers, as they remained on the plantations far longer than Chinese and Japanese immigrants.[92]

In response to laborers deserting jobs, the Hawaiian legislature passed the Masters and Servants Act of 1850 (discussed in chapter 1), with the intention of tying workers to plantations for fixed terms of service.[93] Although the government continued to tighten the laws and practices to exert even more control over the lives of workers, the importation of

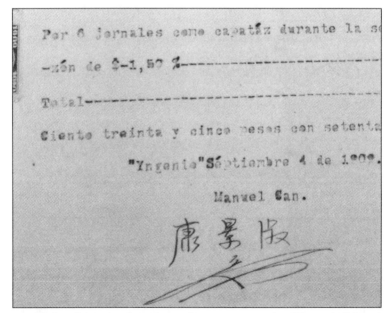

**FIGURE 2.** Receipt in the amount of 135.75 pesos signed in Chinese by Manuel Can. (Photograph by John R. Gust.)

foreign labor by companies virtually ceased when indenture was out-lawed. The workers could not afford passage, and it was too expensive for employers to pay for their travel to Hawai'i if they were not obligated to work for a specified term.[94] Asians (and any others who did not have or were not eligible for U.S. citizenship) were barred from management and skilled positions by the HSPA in 1904.[95]

Dominican sugar growers faced similar labor shortages, and despite anti-immigrant violence, by the 1930s, West Indians replaced Domini-cans in the cane fields and Haitians replaced the West Indians as a major-ity of the harvest workforce.[96] Growers who transported sugar workers were justifiably fearful of the growing prosperity of other parts of the Dominican economy, as Haitian immigrants would much rather work in better-paying and less-brutal occupations. The government responded to this fear and economic change with initiatives that restricting Haitians to working in the sugar industry.[97]

In Yucatán, the overwhelming majority of workers at sugar haciendas were Maya, although there is some indication that a small number of immigrant laborers were working on sugar haciendas. For example, during our archival research, John Gust located labor receipts from the site of San Eusebio in Quintana Roo that were signed in Chinese (figure 2) and Korean. In addition to generally being paid less than Maya work-ers, we also know that hacienda owners often refused to loan money to immigrants, as they feared they might flee, given their lack of ties to the local region.[98]

## ALCOHOL USE AMONG PLANTATION AND HACIENDA LABORERS

Across the Americas, the importation of foreign laborers and slaves left an indelible mark on those countries and cultures. The resulting mix of African peoples we see in the Caribbean and South America today indicate that colonizers took people from various points along the West African coast.[99] This resulted in a diaspora of African peoples, whose cultural practices were blended in the New World in places like Barba-dos, Jamaica, Hispaniola, Trinidad, Cuba, Brazil, and the United States. Among some African groups enslaved in the Caribbean, alcohol was an integral component of their ritual life. The pouring of alcohol con-nected earthly and spiritual planes, was a fundamental part of marriage ceremonies, and strengthened group cohesion.[100] Starting in the sixteenth century, Europeans introduced distilled alcohol into local African religions, using it as a kind of currency.[101] This tradition survived the Middle Passage, although it was the landholding class that controlled access to liquor in the New World.[102] Though alcohol was a linchpin in the maintenance of social identity for the enslaved, slave owners used it as an important tool of control, in part due to its addictive properties. Owners provided it as a weekly ration, and as a reward for the completion of particularly nasty jobs, like clubbing rats in the cane fields, or even for sexual favors.[103] Yet alcohol could also work against slave owners. Social cohesion among coerced laborers became a problem for planters when it contributed to resistance against the system.[104] Slaves and peasants engaged in uprisings in the Caribbean sealed oaths with alcoholic drinks, and celebrations sometimes included the dismemberment of victims and the mixing of their blood with alcohol for consumption.[105]

Although hacienda owners and elites in Yucatán criticized Maya laborers for their drunkenness, they made aguardiente readily available in the company stores. Further, they paid workers in company scrip, thus forcing them to buy their supplies on-site.[106] Haciendas were cash poor and often worked on tight margins.[107] Company stores could also buy rum at by-the-barrel prices and sell it at by-the-bottle prices, increasing their profits while also increasing the workers' debts.[108]

Another strategy that ensured permanent indebtedness across generations of hacienda laborers included the owners supplying children with aguardiente—initially without cost. The hacendado would give young boys crude rum, encouraging them to develop a taste for it. By the time that they were old enough to borrow money, and fully understand the consequences of such borrowing, they would already be addicted. Hacienda owners made small loans that quickly trapped the boys on the hacienda permanently. While Wells and Joseph do not discuss it specifically in this context, the strategy of shifting debts between two sets of books could also be employed to hide the indebtedness of a worker as he indulged his growing taste for rum.[109] It is unclear how widespread this practice of supplying young boys with liquor was, but it does seem particularly insidious.

Furthermore, the rule of law did little to discourage drunkenness. Drunkenness was a mitigating factor in criminal behavior, and people were found not guilty for acts that they committed while intoxicated. This may have caused some defendants to exaggerate memory loss or overstress their inebriated state in the hopes they would receive a reduced sentence. It also gave workers tacit permission to speak to hacienda owners and staff in ways that would result in a lesser punishment than if the workers said the same things while sober.[110] This may have been because it was a kind of pressure release, perhaps reducing the need for collective actions like work slowdowns and revolts.[111] When arrested for drunkenness or other minor crimes off the hacienda grounds, the debt peon was usually released to the hacienda owner because he was integral to keeping the hacienda running. Punishments usually involved whippings to prevent the laborer from spending work hours in jail cells on the hacienda grounds.[112] Worker availability would have trumped other considerations, as the labor requirements of sugarcane cultivation were some of the most intense of any major commodity being produced in the Americas.

Throughout this chapter, we have looked at the similarities and differences among nineteenth-century sugar plantations and rum distilleries across the Americas, including sugar haciendas of the Yucatán Peninsula. Although there was variation in labor patterns in terms of the use of slavery versus debt peonage, differential reliance on immigrant labor following abolition, and the scale of sugar and rum production, there were consistencies in terms of the tendencies of owners and growers to use the system to their advantage. This includes patterns during slavery and debt peonage, as well as after their abolition. And yet there were multiple examples of laborers demonstrating acts of resistance within the context of these forced conditions, including work refusals, threats of allowing crops to rot, or using drunkenness as an excuse for acting out or talking back to supervisors. In chapter 3, will further explore the nature of labor on haciendas in the Yucatán Peninsula under Spanish colonialism.

# CHAPTER 3

# LABORING IN THE YUCATÁN PENINSULA

WHILE IT IS EASY TO assume that the Spanish conquest of Mesoamerica represented an immediate sea change that disrupted the lives of all Indigenous peoples, the reality is far more complex.[1] For Maya peoples, their original social system was left intact, but with the Spanish at its apex. Instead of being immediately deposed, Maya nobility were left in place as tribute collectors and were allowed to retain some of their previous privilege.[2] Their eventual impoverishment was a slow and uneven process that arguably was not completed until the end of the Caste War of the Yucatán Peninsula (1847–1901). The erosion of noble status was driven by changes to the system, by which the Spanish extracted surplus goods and labor from the Maya populace. This chapter chronicles the development of various institutions that colonizers imposed upon Maya people of the Yucatán Peninsula to coerce them to provide unremunerated, or poorly remunerated, goods and services. These institutions were built on previous labor traditions as landowning elites adapted to current worker availability, land scarcity, and market demands at a given time. This culminated in the system of debt peonage on haciendas that lasted until the Mexican Revolution reached the peninsula in 1914.

In the Yucatán Peninsula, including our study area of the north coast of Quintana Roo, each region and individual hacienda adapted the debt peonage to their particular situations. The factors affecting this could be the size of the hacienda, whether the hacienda owners lived on-site, local gender ratios, the amount of nonhacienda lands available to potential peons, the frequency of crop failure, access to foreign workers, the level of capitalization of the hacienda, and the location of the hacienda respective to frontier and/or rebel-held territory. Thus, although henequen haciendas and sugar haciendas could vary in size and complexity across the peninsula, we can use them as points of comparison to thoroughly explore how these operations worked in colonial Yucatán.

## COLONIAL YUCATÁN

The labor and political systems of the Yucatán Peninsula were set up to structurally disenfranchise the working class, especially Indigenous inhabitants.[3] This started with the expropriation of Indigenous lands during the conquest (ca. 1525) and continued with the encomienda system (ca. 1525–1785). The encomienda was a tribute- and labor-based system that granted encomenderos, a predetermined amount of labor and the resulting products, from the Indigenous populace.[4] While the European imposition of the encomienda system was new, it actually paralleled Maya tributary practices in which elites had the right to demand unpaid goods and labor from the populace. This represented the incorporation of Maya traditions into the world economy, however involuntary that incorporation may have been.[5] Thus the encomienda system was the start of globalization on the Yucatán Peninsula.

Two other colonial institutions that operated as vehicles to extract wealth through forced labor were the repartimiento and *repartimiento de mercancías*. The repartimiento was instituted as part of the new laws of 1542 but did not operate in the Yucatán region until the early seventeenth century.[6] While the repartimiento was largely a successor institution to the encomienda elsewhere in México, in the Yucatán Peninsula both systems operated in tandem until the encomienda system was abolished in 1785.[7] A repartimiento holder was given land along with rights over the Indigenous people living on it. This meant they could extract limited and intermittent labor from Indigenous peoples.[8] Generally, under the repartimiento de mercancías, elites compelled Indigenous people to buy luxury goods that they did not want at high prices. The system varied within the Spanish Empire, but across Mesoamerica, this usually meant that native people were advanced a line of credit that then had to be paid back, usually in the form of labor.[9] Due to the two different forms of repartimiento and their different regional expressions, Indigenous peoples became the producers of raw materials for low wages, the involuntary producers of finished goods, and the purchasers of luxury goods against their will.[10]

Further, the issue of land ownership was complicated in New Spain. Spanish royalty had enough experience operating in Spain to understand the threat that a new class of Spanish nobility posed to them. The Crown wanted the former conquistadors to remain dependent and instituted rules to ensure this.[11] Instead of granting perpetual land grants in the New World, the Crown made certain that they expired with the death of the grantee. This helped ensure fealty (a feudal tenant's loyalty) during the life of the grantee.[12] While grants were often resold to the next generation of the same family, they had to first prove their allegiance.[13] Other, sometimes landless, Spaniards loyal to the Crown could vie to receive the lands. This helped safeguard against new nobility cementing itself into place in Spanish colonies.[14]

The threat of this new nobility class also contributed to standards on the treatment of Indigenous populations. Although there were Spaniards who genuinely thought that the native populations should be treated "fairly," this was not the only impetus for laws governing treatment. By limiting how much Maya peoples (and other Indigenous groups throughout New Spain) could be forced to produce, the Spanish Crown was still able to extract a handsome tribute while restricting the power of elites in México.[15]

Meanwhile, Yucatecan elites searched for decades for a viable and profitable industry that could be run on a large scale. The Yucatán Peninsula has rocky, thin, and easily exhaustible soils, coupled with a total lack of surface rivers in the northern half of the peninsula.[16] This represented an important natural impediment to most cash-crop agriculture, especially in the northeast corner of the region.[17] Although local Maya farmers learned to grow a wide array of plants for subsistence use, the particularities of the terrain made most cash cropping unfeasible. While Spaniards attempted sugar production as early as 1540, once the powerful Montejo family was stripped of its encomienda, the industry was abandoned.[18] Similarly, indigo dye lost importance after the boom times of the second half of the sixteenth century ended. Further, because the Spanish could extract tribute payments from the crops that Maya farmers grew, it was in their best interest to keep them farming on these marginal lands.[19]

However, the Spanish need for large tracts of land grew as they entered into industrial agriculture in the form of small-scale cattle ranches, or estancias. Patch reports from 1718 to 1738 that the median number of cattle was only 87 head, that one quarter of estancias had 21 or fewer head, and that the highest quartile had 180 to 263 head.[20] Only three estancias grew crops, which in all cases was maize.[21] The staffing needs at estancias were also very low, so they did not require extraordinary measures to attract and retain multitudes of Indigenous workers. Of the fifty-three estancias for which records were available, only five included debts for peons.[22]

Before 1750, grain shortages occurred when there was a general crop failure. By 1750, Maya populations began to rebound from the impacts of war and disease and continued to increase until 1847.[23] With this increased population pressure, mediocre harvests resulted in grain shortages and crop failures produced famine.[24] This was compounded with an expansion of the estancia sector of the economy to meet high demands for beef in Veracruz, México, and Havana, Cuba. Although this created a necessity for labor drafts, only enough people were hired to produce export goods, at the cost of local shortages for foodstuffs like rice.[25] An example of this is the comparison of sugar/aguardiente[26] production versus grain production in the Yucatán Peninsula in the eighteenth century. In 1750, approximately 40 percent of the imports coming into Yucatán through the port of Sisal were sugar and aguardiente.[27] While planters in what is now Campeche sought to meet this demand, in the 1770s the Spanish Crown tried to limit localized sugar production by enacting the "*estanco de aguardiente.*" This was aimed at stopping the export of sugar from Campeche into Yucatán, in response to complaints from competing producers[28] elsewhere in the Spanish Empire. Meanwhile, the sugar and rum industry in Yucatán demanded more workers than could be supplied, leaving only a few nonnatives to produce grain.[29]

The Spanish Crown officially banned aguardiente production until 1796, although they allowed limited imports from Cuba[30] and small illegal stills were common wherever sugarcane was grown.[31] With the increase in the size of estancias and the growing importance of haciendas, land became scarcer as Maya and Spanish tried to acquire and/or hold as much land as possible. The Spanish thus began to rely on *luneros,* who were usually Maya laborers, who worked one day a week—typically Mondays (from *lunes,* Spanish for Monday).[32] Luneros started as free laborers who traded a day's work for access to land for growing milpa.[33] As free laborers, the landowners could not punish luneros or require cash payments for access to land, and they could only expel them if they believed the lunero had not lived up to their side of the bargain.[34] Haciendas allowed luneros to construct new agricultural centers, which was an added benefit for them. These centers would have otherwise been established in secret and in violation of the practice of *reduccion*, which had been concentrating people in larger settlements that often held too few lands.[35] Luneros, however, did not receive the benefits of peonage, as they were still expected to pay taxes, complete *fajina* labor for their community, and provide obligatory military service.[36] For a time, landowners preferred the lunero system over debt peonage, opting for the limited responsibility of simply providing land to farm.[37] Landowners protested a proposed law that would have made them pay the luneros' taxes and attached these laborers to the estate.[38] However, in 1786 landholders were made responsible for lunero taxes, and by 1813 the amount of labor service had doubled, effectively converting the lunero system into debt peonage and raising the ire of the upper class.[39]

## THE CASTE WAR AND ITS UNDERPINNINGS

Beginning in 1810, Mexican elites initiated a war for independence from Spain.[40] After more than ten years of fighting against Spanish forces and loyalist Mexicans, México achieved independence from Spain on September 27, 1821. Although the revolution emphasized the rights of Indigenous peoples, following independence, the elites of México moved to lift the limits that the Spanish Crown had imposed on their treatment of México's Indigenous inhabitants.[41] The strategies that they used varied by region, as did the Indigenous peoples' responses to these strategies. In the Yucatán Peninsula, they dissolved the existing land tenure system, in which most lands were held communally by towns and villages. In the past, the town government granted access to land in exchange for providing community labor. After Mexican independence, the size of communal lands was significantly curtailed and other lands were privatized, as 134,000 hectares were removed from Indigenous hands.[42] By 1843, the lunero was virtually nonexistent and luneros were all but indistinguishable from other peons.[43] The primarily Maya workforce had few options. They could (a) try to cultivate the limited land that was available to them and either avoid or assent to the required yearly military service, (b) become a resident peon, or (c) choose to flee.[44] While many fled to the east coast of the peninsula, to what is now the state of Quintana Roo, some residents resorted to peonage.[45] Katz defines debt peonage as "a form of forced labor, which develops when a number of social and economic prerequisites for bondage in agriculture (such as a powerful group of large landowners, a shortage of labor, etc.) exists but the state officially refuses to implement bondage while tacitly tolerating and acknowledging it under another name."[46]

Once workers were attached to an hacienda, the owner, or hacendado, dominated their lives, punishing them with extra (unpaid) work and beating them for even small infractions.[47] The labor regimes of the Yucatán Peninsula were influenced by external forces demanding cash-crop commodities rather than the internal needs of the region (i.e., feeding the populace), resulting in the mass exploitation of workers.[48] Throughout the 1840s, the debt peonage system became more solidified and more onerous. Florescano has observed that while the workers were technically free, they lived without freedom of movement.[49] As land became scarcer, it was difficult for the lower class to avoid becoming indebted. Once sufficiently indebted, workers had to ask permission to leave the hacienda (figure 3) until their debts were paid off. Lack of mobility and payment in company scrip meant that workers and their families had to buy needed supplies from the company store, sometimes at high markups.[50] In 1843,

**FIGURE 3.** Main house and grounds of Hacienda Nohchakan, located near Cuzama, Yucatán. (Photograph by John R. Gust.)

the Yucatecan government officially recognized the right of hacienda owners to use peonage as a bonding mechanism, making it easy to entrap workers into a cycle of debt for their lifetimes.[51] This same law also barred peons from being employed elsewhere if they left without paying their debts and granted haciendas legal authority on some judicial matters. Working conditions varied by hacienda, but involved working long hours for low wages in a hot environment. Workers cleared land, weeded, and harvested crops like henequen or sugarcane using sharp machetes or cane knives. Harvests were processed with machinery that could easily result in deadly burns or limb entanglement. Beyond official tasks, uncompensated maintenance and domestic work was expected of workers and their families. In the context of these conditions, the Caste War started on July 30, 1847, with Cecilio Chi of Tepich initially in command of the largely Maya forces.[52] The rebellious forces swept through the countryside, freeing workers from servitude and sometimes killing or capturing the owners and their families. While land loss was a major issue, seizures did not directly predict the likelihood that a settlement would participate in a revolt.[53] Those Maya engaged in revolt participated in skirmishes and larger battles as they moved north and west, recruiting new fighters as they traveled. Both sides of the conflict raided pueblos and villages as they moved, looking for traitors to the respective causes and seizing supplies. Rebel leaders, rank-and-file soldiers, and battlefield fighters committed acts of brutality within their respective strongholds.[54]

A side effect of the Caste War was that it ended ambitions of independence among Yucatán's elite from México. Facing defeat by the rebels in 1848, the government of the Yucatán Peninsula sought and received military aid from the Mexican government at the price of permanently rejoining the Republic.[55] By the mid-1850s, the Mexican and Yucatecan armies controlled most of the peninsula, while the rebels flourished in Chan Santa Cruz, now known as Felipe Carrillo Puerto (map 3). The rebels or insurgents were known as the *cruceros*, a name derived from their adherence to what became known as the "Cult of the Talking Cross." During major hostilities, rebel leaders said that a cross, often described as floating and/or draped in blue fabric, talked to them, counseling them on the next steps that they should take as they executed the war.[56] Chan Santa Cruz became a defensible position for holdout rebels and a base from which raiding could originate. While no longer a peninsula-wide threat after the mid-1850s, the continuing belligerence of the Santa Cruz Maya was a source of political, social, and economic instability. After completing a raid,

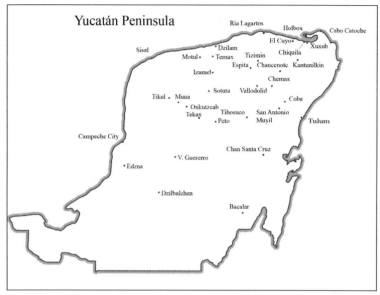

**MAP 3.** The Yucatán Peninsula. (Map by John R. Gust.)

the rebels would retreat to the relative safety of the remote Chan Santa Cruz area. Thus, even after major hostilities ended, the cruceros effectively threatened commerce and the safety of local landowners, until they were finally defeated militarily by government forces in 1901.[57]

As with most conflicts, there were multiple perspectives on the Caste War. The peninsular government and their primarily white supporters wanted to remain in control and needed a pliant working class in order to rebuild destroyed cities, towns, and haciendas.[58] The cruceros hoped to free the peninsula of whites, often saying that they wanted to push them into the sea.[59] There was not universal support for the rebellion among the Indigenous and laboring populace that the uprising was intended to free. The allied Yucatecan and Mexican forces and the Maya rebels both seized needed supplies from the populace to supply their troops and continue fighting.[60] Some groups of Maya and other lower-class people moved south toward current-day Belize to avoid the conflict. War weariness among the general populace led some villages and towns, primarily on the periphery, to settle with the government of Yucatán, pledging military support in exchange for protection and peace in the 1850s.[61] For example, community members in Kantunilkin, the largest town near the north coast of Quintana Roo, formed a pact with the Yucatecan government in 1855.[62] Agreements such as this, in addition to resupplying issues, led to the rebels being pushed out of northwestern and central areas of the peninsula. This meant a return to some level of normalcy for these now peaceful communities. They had limited autonomy but were free to farm without the constant threat of their fields being raided or burned.[63]

Strategically, these peace agreements benefited the government, as large forces were no longer needed to control the area. Government forces acquired uneasy allies, but the rebels saw the townspeople as traitors to the cause of ridding the peninsula of the European oppressors. With the interests of the government and pacified towns now intersecting, the majority of military units could be redeployed into hot zones. This left small garrisons or even sheriffs with limited forces and temporary volunteers in charge of keeping the peace. In some cases, townspeople such as those in Kantunilkin cooperated with government forces and even took up arms against rebels because they now saw them as the more dangerous enemy.[64]

Although the Caste War failed to force the whites out of Yucatán, it did succeed in slowing the expansion of haciendas for about ten years. Nonetheless, the situation for Maya and other nonelites outside rebel-held territory further deteriorated.[65] Now even more powerful, elites

**FIGURE 4.** Worker weeding a field of henequen plants at Ruinas de Ake, Yucatán. (Copyright Macduff Everton 2019, image 16970.)

searched for new and greater sources of income. One of the cash crops landowners turned to was henequen, a fiber-producing species of agave that the Maya had used for centuries (figure 4).[66]

The invention of the rasping machine (figure 5) in 1862 allowed workers to more easily free the fiber from henequen leaves.[67] Much like Eli Whitney's gin in the U.S. cotton industry, the rasping machine efficiently separated the desired fiber from the waste parts of the plant, thereby significantly reducing production costs.[68] In the United States in the 1870s, the invention of the McCormick Reaper for harvesting and binding grain crops led to an increased demand for henequen as a biodegradable twine. Farmers needed a supply that was reliable, and "[h]enequen's three- to four-foot long fibers and general imperviousness to disease and pestilence fulfilled that need perfectly."[69] Demand increased from six million kilos in 1875 to eighty-one million kilos by the turn of the century.[70] The International Harvester Company imported almost all of its crop to the United States,[71] and Yucatán's "green gold" transformed "one of the poorest states in the republic to one of the richest."[72] When Porfirio Díaz became president of México, he instituted policies that exerted more pressure on the Maya people, including privatizing more land for cash cropping and increasing the debts of workers, further attaching them to the haciendas.[73]

Gilbert Joseph, Allen Wells, and their colleagues recount in great detail the rise and fall of many of the henequen export houses.[74] The northwest portion of the peninsula emerged as the center of henequen cultivation, placing Yucatán's most important export commodity near its seat of power in Mérida, the capital of Yucatán. In 1902, Olegario Molina y Compania became International Harvester's sole supplier, the same year Olegario Molina was elected governor of Yucatán.[75] As the dual roles held by Molina illustrate, economic elites were often also political elites.[76] Local leadership thus helped ensure that crops would be safely transported to the largest ports, making it profitable for a small henequen oligarchy dubbed the "*Casta Divina*," or Divine Caste.[77]

Consolidation of the export supply generally only benefited the Olegario Molina y Compania. Before consolidation, producers could negotiate with export companies for the best price for their crops or request production loans that acted to smooth out supply shocks, adding a measure of predictability to the economics of agricultural production.[78] With consolidation, however, many growers were contracted with the Olegario Molina y Compania, making it impossible to affect price by withholding

**FIGURE 5.** Worker hanging henequen (sisal) fiber emerging from rasping machine in Holactun, Yucatán. (Copyright Macduff Everton 2019, image 12450.)

supply.[79] Further, numerous owners held haciendas as collateral for other business dealings or lived as absentee owners, funding a life of luxury in cities such as Mérida.[80] The added pressure of tight credit for henequen production, due to supply consolidation, made borrowing against haciendas even more necessary. Smaller operations were sold to wealthy hacendados either by their owners or by lien holders after being seized.[81] This resulted in fewer but larger haciendas and multiple haciendas under single ownership by the late nineteenth century.[82]

## THE PORFIRIAN HENEQUEN HACIENDA

Muckraking journalists, archaeologists, and historians have written on the Porfirian henequen haciendas of Yucatán, presenting a wide array of perspectives of what life was like there.[83] Scholars such as Alston and colleagues advocate for taking a middle path between those that they consider apologists of the system and critics that view the system as pure exploitation.[84] Our survey of the literature leads us to believe that debt peonage existed on a continuum between paternalistic exploitation and pure exploitation. Specific conditions at any given hacienda were based on the character of particular hacendados and their managerial staff. The purpose of this section is to discuss the varying practices deployed at different henequen haciendas and provide points of comparison for how labor was managed at sugar production operations during the nineteenth century in Quintana Roo. The following discussion is structured by the following five questions:

1. What were the normal working conditions for those laboring on haciendas?
2. What led a worker to be indebted, and once entrapped, what mechanisms kept a peon from paying his debts?
3. What mechanisms were (and were not) used to make peonage de facto hereditary?
4. What responsibilities did other members of the family have under peonage?
5. What were the wages for indebted peons and other workers employed by haciendas?

## WHAT WERE THE NORMAL WORKING CONDITIONS FOR THOSE LABORING ON HACIENDAS?

This simple question becomes much harder to answer when we consider that henequen haciendas operated as factory farms, in which various job assignments had distinct working conditions. The general categories of workers were managers and laborers that earned a salary (daily or weekly), and laborers that worked at piece rates, called *jornaleros*. The salaried workforce was mostly Mestizo (mixed race), while the jornaleros were usually Maya, although Mestizo jornaleros did exist and had a better chance of upward mobility on the hacienda.[85] Working henequen was hot and dangerous work. Managers expected piece-rate laborers in the fields to weed 1–2 mecates of land a day, or to cut and dress 2,000–2,500 agave leaves.[86] They had little to no protective gear and had to use large, sharp tools to cut the spiny leaves.[87] Back at the processing house, workers often got limbs or clothing caught in the rasping machines (see figure 5), leading to injuries.[88] This was exacerbated by the fact that workers were paid based on production and were likely to work too quickly. Alternatively, the pay system did not always work effectively to spur high output, as workers were sometimes beaten for production shortfalls or laziness.[89]

The length of the workday itself does appear to have varied widely. Rejón Patrón reports that the workday for jornaleros was fourteen to fifteen hours long during the harvest season.[90] The hacendados also demanded up to two hours per day, except Sundays, of unpaid fajina labor that usually involved maintenance of the hacienda grounds and facilities. While Maya workers were accustomed to laboring to benefit their own communities, the hacendados usurped this tradition to promote their own needs.[91] Depending on whether this two-hour period is included in the above estimate, the actual workday could have been as long as seventeen hours during certain times of the year. The number of itinerant wage workers versus indebted debt peons also varied through time and by location.

Another factor affecting labor conditions is whether or not an individual worked on the hacienda full-time. Part-time jornalero workers were the most abused: "One such 'part-timer' told [John Kenneth] Turner that it was certainly preferable to work as a permanent peon. As regards part-timers like himself, he added, 'they work us until we are ready to fall, and then they throw us away to get strong again. If they worked the full-timers like they work us they would die."'[92] Hacendados may have intentionally held a group of workers with only moderate debts, in order to employ them part-time for harder work at the same base rate. Conversely, avoiding this harsher work may have been a reason to borrow enough debt to become a full-time worker. When becoming a resident debt peon was an option, the worker had to weigh the benefits of better working conditions against the detriment of the loss of autonomy.

## WHAT LED A WORKER TO BE INDEBTED, AND ONCE ENTRAPPED, WHAT MECHANISMS KEPT A PEON FROM PAYING HIS DEBTS?

The nature of henequen production was labor-intensive, and hacienda owners were always in need of more workers. Although some workers wanted to remain unattached, hacendados put a concerted effort and material expenditure into binding them to the hacienda. First, the hacendado offered "generous" loans to pay for expensive festivals—especially weddings.[93] Maya have a long tradition of elaborate weddings and usually married at a relatively young average age.[94] This meant that a wedding loan could ensnare workers into a debt cycle that started in their mid-teens and continued until their deaths.

Fallaw reports that cantina owners would alert hacendados to patrons with high bar tabs and the hacendado would offer loans to pay them off.[95] Second, access to land was often contingent upon Maya workers being indebted to an hacienda owner, although it is unclear what level of indebtedness was necessary to gain access to land.[96] Third, workers were often forced to shop on-site at the expensive company store (*tienda de raya*) for their daily needs. In particular, during times of local crop failure and famine, haciendas might be the only place where people, including those unattached to an hacienda, could buy food. By controlling scarce food supplies, hacendados left many families with the choice of buying expensive food on credit or starving. Thus, for the price of a single season's worth of food, a worker became indebted for life.[97] A fourth way that hacendados entrapped workers was by using two sets of books to record debt. The hacienda owner would order that separate books be kept for large loans and small purchases. Small loans for day-to-day needs would be kept in the book known as the *chichan cuenta*, and larger loans were held in the *nohoch cuenta*. Moving debts between the two books obscured the worker's level of indebtedness, as the worker might be less prone to be thrifty in their purchases.[98] A fifth method of entrapment was deception. The working classes usually had minimal, if any, education and may not have understood basic accounting principles. Some hacendados falsified debt ledgers by inflating amounts owed or failed to record payments made against the debt. The hacendados and their staff controlled the ledgers and could make changes without informing the workers.[99] Lastly, under the law, independent farmers and other unattached workers had to pay their own taxes and do so in currency, not trade. Even successful, independent milpa farmers lacked the cash to pay these taxes and took out loans from hacendados against future crops. They became indebted when their crops failed, their property was seized for nonpayment, and thus they were pushed onto haciendas or accepted peonage as a last resort.[100]

The number of resident peons as a percentage of the populace grew significantly, from 9.46 percent in 1885 to 32.24 percent in 1910.[101] As Meyers and Carlson discuss:

> Debt was essential to power relations on the hacienda, as the amount of debt often determined the servant's freedom of movement. Some haciendas . . . even established categories of debt in the late nineteenth century to mandate the amount of labor required by the worker. . . . Those who had less than 100 pesos of debt were classified as temporary workers. They were required to work for a single, specified period of time, usually during the harvest season. Individuals with a debt of 100–200 pesos had to work every other week for the hacienda. Servants with over 200 pesos of debt had to work every day except Sunday, and they were prohibited from leaving the estate without consent of their supervisors. The majority of resident laborers easily surpassed the requisite 200 pesos of debt needed to mandate full-time work on the estate. . . . [A loan for their wedding] could secure an individual's obligation to work perennially on the hacienda and eliminate his family's freedom.[102]

The amounts of the loans made to the debt peons are still puzzling, in that they were often much larger than would have been necessary to tie the peon to the hacienda for life. One interpretation is that the overages could essentially be gifts or acts of paternal benevolence on the part of the hacendados. This engendered what Alston and colleagues term "loyal-like behavior" among the debt peons, which acted to stabilize the workforce.[103] An alternative hypothesis is that a worker could demand his *carta cuenta* (an accounting of his debts) at any time, and attempt to convince another owner to buy their debt, allowing the peon to switch haciendas.[104] However, a peon with higher debts would be less attractive to another hacienda owner, diminishing the possibility that the worker would leave his lands. The counter to these hypotheses, though, is that eventually a fluctuating price emerged in payment for a debt peon to leave his hacienda, irrespective of the debt actually owed. As Katz puts it, in the classic system of debt peonage, when a peon wanted to transfer from one hacienda to another, his new master had to assume his debt.[105] When an hacienda was sold, these debts were added up. In Yucatán this practice, though existent in theory, had been superseded by another. The peon's value was decided by a market price independent of the peon's debt but very much dependent on general market conditions, especially on the price of sisal. Around 1895, the price of a peon was quoted at between two and three hundred pesos. In 1900, with a sharp rise in the price of sisal, the price of a worker rose to between 1,500 and 3,000 pesos. After the crisis of 1907, it fell back to 400 pesos.

This shows that the hacendados expected that debt peons would never be able to pay back their debts, but more importantly, leads to questions about the debt peonage system itself. Debt peonage is argued to not be enslavement because it is not based on ownership of the peon but on ownership of the debt. By divorcing the price for a peon to leave an hacienda from that debt, what is actually being sold is rights to the peon himself. Under true slavery, the expectation would be that an individual slave would be valued based on his or her perceived or proven ability to produce. The set price confounds this expectation as well. Thus, arguably in some areas, the debt peonage system morphed into a hybrid system taking on even more of the character of true chattel slavery, and also introducing new elements not seen in either system.

## WHAT MECHANISMS WERE (AND WERE NOT) USED TO MAKE PEONAGE DE FACTO HEREDITARY?

As Rivero notes, the hacendados were inclined to ensure that future generations stayed indebted to the hacienda, reproducing unequal power relations.[106] Rivero reports that on some haciendas, when adolescent boys and girls reached marriageable age, the hacendados arranged unions for them by lining up the young women and allowing the young man to choose one.[107] Usually the unions were marriages between people from two haciendas owned by the same family, or the result of bride exchange between allied hacienda-owning families. The wedding ceremonies were usually costly, necessitating a loan from the hacendado to the young man (or his future bride), who then became an indebted peon, probably even before he was fully grown.[108] Indebted parents would likely not have funds to help a son leave the hacienda and set up a new life elsewhere. If a son was to leave through use of a loan, he would be a debt peon, but without the benefit of being with his family. Arranged marriages sometimes also crossed generational boundaries, as in the case of the death of a first spouse. In those cases, an older man might marry the sister of his son's wife, thus becoming his own son's brother-in-law.[109] It is easy to see how this cycle was self-replicating.

Perhaps surprisingly, despite these attempts to encourage peonage, the debts themselves were not generally passed from father to son when someone died.[110] The reason for not using this seemingly simple way to trap new generations of workers is not discussed in the literature. Perhaps it was seen as both inflammatory to the worker and unnecessary.

## WHAT RESPONSIBILITIES DID OTHER MEMBERS OF THE FAMILY HAVE UNDER PEONAGE?

Thus far, our discussion has centered almost entirely around peon men and boys. Unfortunately, our discussion of women in this chapter is brief, as they are rarely represented in the historical or archaeological records. Men are most often treated in the existing documents as the responsible party for the household, and while wives and daughters are implied as part of that household, they are rarely discussed. Women and children often suffered abuse from husbands and fathers who drunkenly released their pent-up frustrations on their families, going without the necessities of life when the wages were spent on alcohol.

In general, the living and working conditions of women were a by-product of their husbands' situations. Men were assigned paid tasks, but in addition to addressing the duties of their own house, resident women and girls were expected to perform uncompensated labor in the planter's house, such as cleaning and cooking.[111] In some cases, men were assigned a task that they could not complete by themselves, and the entire family helped out.[112] The male head of household would receive the pay and would then control its distribution. The extent to which others would benefit would be based on the temperament of the head of household. This implies that the full piece rate was really conceived as a family wage. Adolescent boys were usually paid half the piece rate for the same work, but appear to have been paid directly.[113]

Older men who could no longer work a full day would receive lighter assignments for less pay and were designated as *reservados*—part of a reserve workforce that could be called on should an acute need for labor present itself.[114] Similarly, nohoch cuenta books and company store receipts for haciendas also included small payments to support widows.[115] The one peso per week grant and ration of corn paid to widows was meager, so presumably women who were young enough to have small children when widowed were encouraged to remarry.[116]

In their investigation of the Colorado Coalfield War, the Ludlow Collective found that the wives and families of coal miners were active and necessary parts of the household economy, and we think that the same would be true for those women and children connected to the hacienda.[117] Failing evidence to the contrary, the most parsimonious explanation is that women were active agents negotiating their situation just as much as their husbands, but gender hierarchy interfered with the documentation of such acts.

Henequen hacienda workers and their families sometimes engaged in outside work to supplement their income.[118] The sporadic nature of growing and harvesting sugarcane made such diversification critical for laborers who lived off the hacienda (see chapter 4).[119] The lower absolute pay rate for worker subsistence that this supplemental work allowed was sometimes "the difference between profitability and ruin for enterprises in peripheral regions such as Yucatán."[120] The standard wages met only basic subsistence, and while in some places these low wages were supplemented with rations, these were often converted into advances.[121]

## WHAT WERE THE WAGES FOR INDEBTED PEONS AND OTHER WORKERS EMPLOYED BY HACIENDAS?

The best-paid laborers on haciendas were the machine operators, followed by the overseers (known as *encargados* and *mayordomos*), and then by "increasing numbers[s] of free technicians."[122] Below these positions were a number of salaried positions, including "cowboys, stablemen, tram-car operators, and *mayocoles* who supervised work-gangs in the fields." These employees all worked for a daily rate that varied based on what job they were assigned for that week or even that day.[123] A "skilled" worker would earn 3.45 to 7.5 pesos per week.[124]

The specifics concerning the length of the workday for the salaried employees are currently unknown. As the jornalero workday varied with the agricultural cycle, we believe that workdays lengthened during the planting and harvest seasons, though it is uncertain to what degree this fluctuated. Employees in certain positions, like tram-car operators, were generally paid for five days of work per week. Other employees, like the *mecanico* and the stablemen, were paid for seven days per week. We think this indicates a working schedule that included normal working hours of some length and an ongoing "on-call" status. These employees would be expected to work whenever problems arose.

Jornaleros were the least-paid and worst-treated workers, especially those that worked on the hacienda part-time or at a piece rate.[125] Task rates varied, but an example from 1907 is a rate of 0.75 pesos per 2,000 henequen leaves cut, dressed, and made ready for rasping.[126] Workers laboring at piece rates made less in absolute terms, with a normal range of 3.5 to 6.5 pesos per week.[127] Their work was also more difficult and less specialized, and when it required the efforts of family members (as discussed previously), it further lowered the comparative pay per person per unit of time.

The ratio of Indigenous workers living in villages compared to Indigenous workers living on haciendas fell steadily from the period before the Caste War and into the Porfiriato, due to land seizures and other restrictions placed on nonelites.[128] Despite this, there were still labor shortages, and haciendas brought in an estimated eight thousand Yaqui Indians from northern México and three thousand East Asians to help supplement the workforce.[129] While these imported workers should have caused downward pressure on all wages, we have not found evidence of this. And yet hacendados did treat these foreign workers differently than workers native to the Yucatán Peninsula. Although hacendados viewed granting loans as a better investment than an increase in wages, they commonly denied loans to imported workers, as they feared that they could flee without repaying their debts.[130]

Planters paid wages in credit (*moneda de cuenta*, or scrip)[131] that was only usable at the *tienda de raya* (the company store).[132] This had several benefits for the hacendados. First, they were able to keep track of the finances of their workers, debt peons, and wage laborers alike. Second, it ensured that if a debt peon was to flee, they would have little cash to take with them. Third, the hacendados were able to socially engineer life on the haciendas by controlling the price of goods. However, although the hacendados could gouge workers on the price of needed goods, they did not always do so.[133] In fact, they sometimes subsidized the prices for commodities like corn, particularly during periods of inflation due to crop failure.[134] This would not only ensure the debt peons would not starve, but as discussed previously, could entice new workers to attach themselves to an hacienda.

## MAYA AGENCY UNDER DEBT PEONAGE

While we might see Maya peoples in Yucatán as victims pushed around by circumstance, this perspective simplifies history and reduces them to something less than fully capable human beings. However, practice theorists Pierre Bourdieu and Anthony Giddens describe how people navigate their lives by making choices within constraints and deciding whether or not to accept those constraints.[135] Acting as agents, people are able to effect the change they want or make life more difficult for those who exploit them.

Maya peoples proved to be formidable rivals to their oppressors. The Spanish conquest of the Maya area was slow in its progress, and there were holdout populations, including at Tayasal until 1697 and the Lacandon Maya of Guatemala, who never surrendered.[136] During the Caste War, Maya fighters came close to ridding the peninsula of the white ruling class, and in so doing dashed the hopes of an independent Yucatán. Once defeated, crucero holdouts occupied and raided from Chan Santa Cruz until 1901, and rebel descendants known as the "Iglesia Maya" are still a political force in the coastal town of Tulum today.[137] As discussed previously, some Maya villages and towns opted to settle with the Yucatecan government in exchange for an end to hostilities with a concession of limited autonomy. Maya are known throughout history as a capable physical threat and used that reputation to make conditions more favorable to them and push back against those who exploited them. Maya villages fought hard to keep their lands against expropriations by hacienda owners.

We can also assume that Maya who accepted loans and became attached to haciendas were making an active choice. Although their other options were dire (such as going hungry or squatting) and they placed themselves in undesirable conditions, Michel de Certeau argues that people can fight against oppressive systems, even if only in small ways.[138] For example, Maya may have negotiated for more in loans than would be necessary to ensure continued attachment to the hacienda and dissuade another hacendado from buying the workers' debts, reducing a chance of upheaval. Further, in hacienda villages, the better housing placements went to the salaried workers, while the older jornaleros and their wives tended to be the most impoverished.[139] While accepting peonage did result in greater poverty in old age compared to those with access to sufficient village lands, it came with a guarantee of some income as a *reservado* for the worker and a limited stipend for a widow. Compared to a life of scraping by on rented land (if any was available), hacienda residency did come with some minimal security in old age.

The most powerful point of resistance for coerced farm workers was refusal to work, foot-dragging, or otherwise impeding the harvest and processing of the sugarcane crop. Harvesttime was a point of particular risk for the planter, when maximum costs were invested in the crop without any return. The possibility of crops rotting in the field or before being processed meant that the effect of work slowdowns, feigned illness, or drunkenness to avoid work was the greatest. This was also the point at which sabotage would be most effective. Workers could maximize losses for the planter by destroying machines or crops just before harvest or setting fire to crops (aiding in the harvest but killing the cane above ground) and then not harvesting it.[140] Even if no sabotage ever occurred, the planter was still forced to expend physical and mental energy guarding against it. Indebted workers who refused to work could be whipped or imprisoned. However, this meant that their work was withdrawn from the system. On occasion, workers chose suicide instead of continuing to work on the hacienda.[141] Although it came at the highest cost to the individual, debts generally died with the debt peon, meaning that this was the ultimate act of defiance against the hacendado.

## PLANTER ABSENTEEISM

One attribute that many plantations and some hacienda owners shared was a desire to live off the farm. For most owners this meant traveling to the United States or Europe, while in the Yucatán Peninsula this usually meant living in the state's capital of Mérida. Living in Mérida was a viable option for many hacienda owners because they could visit weekly or at least multiple times per year while overseeing their various investments in urban comfort, leaving day-to-day management of the hacienda to a hired manager.[142] The relatively short distance between the hacienda and the city no doubt made owners feel in control of their assets while living in the city. In one case, a wealthy Yucatecan owner by the name of Ramón Aznar had massive land holdings near Mérida, but agreed to buy the sugar hacienda of Xuxub in a remote area of Quintana Roo when Robert Stephens agreed to live on-site and manage the operations for a decade. Aznar was thus able to live in a large colonnaded estate on his hacienda grounds in Yucatán state, but could still grow his wealth in Quintana Roo under Stephens's tenure.[143]

Many of the Caribbean sugar planters wanted to show off their new wealth back home; however, the economic margins for sugar production made this possible for only the richest owners.[144] Residing in or traveling in Europe itself represented living costs that were greater compared to living on the plantation. This absenteeism also meant that plantation managers could enrich themselves at the expense of the operation's profits.[145] Slower communication and inability of the owner to visit periodically made it much easier for the manager to focus more on their personal finances than on those of the plantation. Absentee planters were often more abusive to their slaves than resident planters, as they tried to squeeze out every penny for their lives off the plantation, while also contending with the graft of their managers. Absentee owners wanted to keep the whole price paid for sugar when it was sold in Europe, so the plant managers had to boost production of rum for sale on the islands. Planters expected to operate the plantation on the sale of rum and molasses, leaving all proceeds from sugar as profit.[146]

## THE MEXICAN REVOLUTION, THE END OF DEBT PEONAGE, AND AGRARIAN REFORM

As a result of the Mexican Revolution of 1910, México outlawed debt peonage in 1914 and abolished the hacienda system in 1917.[147] Yet economic conditions for freed debt peons were difficult, as the result was the decline of the paternalistic elements of peonage without restoration of the means to make a living. For free laborers, employer-provided housing was gone or contingent on continued employment, and health care was now the responsibility of the worker.[148] Freed former debt peons were also slow to receive the land they were promised. Lastly, the impetus to loan Maya workers money for celebrations was diminished, as was any reason for plantation owners to expend extra money at Christmas.[149] Military governor of Yucatán, General Salvador Alvarado, sought to eliminate the wealth gaps between henequen farmers and the rural poor, but also needed a working henequen industry and had suppressed popular uprisings between 1911 and 1915.[150] Because of this lack of sustained revolt in Yucatán, Ben W. Fallaw and Gilbert Joseph refer to the Mexican Revolution in Yucatán as a "revolution from without." While the lower class of benefited when the revolutionary army came to Yucatán, they did not contribute significantly to fighting in the war.[151] Alvarado sought to "Mexicanize" the Indigenous population in order to save them from "poverty, alcoholism, and social isolationism," and had no interest in furthering Maya practice or Mayan-language instruction in schools.[152] This tension between indigeneity as backward and a stumbling block to advancement versus indigeneity as a vehicle for positive change is seen in the programs of subsequent Yucatecan leaders.[153] Alvarado's successor, Felipe Carrillo Puerto (1922–24), tried "to encourage ethnic pride as a means of eventually instilling class consciousness, *indigenismo* being merely a way-station on the road to socialism."[154] He also supported the restoration of Maya sites as a method of instilling ethnic pride.[155]

The nature and magnitude of reforms was a point of contention among the leaders of the Mexican Revolution. Emiliano Zapata and Pancho Villa pushed for more radical land redistribution and other reforms aimed to strip the entrenched oligarchy that had ruled México of their holdings. The Constitutionalists had seen promises of reform as a necessary part of the success of the revolution but were not ideologically bound to it.[156] When the Constitutionalists defeated Zapata (ambushed and murdered in 1919) and Villa (assassinated in 1923), the result was a more conservative redistribution of hacienda land.[157] This established communal land holding units known as ejidos, which left many villages, and therefore individual Maya, with too little land to farm.[158] In part, this was because most of this ejido land was composed of woodlands that owners perceived to have poor agricultural potential. As the seized land was not farmland, and because many haciendas had converted processing equipment to liquid fuel and did not need significant amounts of firewood, these losses did not significantly disrupt henequen operations.[159]

In the late 1930s, a second round of redistribution known as the agrarian reform further stripped hacendados of lands, though still not to the degree that had been promised by Mexican president Lázaro Cárdenas (1934–40).[160] In 1937, the maximum size of an hacienda was reduced to three hundred hectares. Many of the recipients of this land continued to plant henequen, and the planter class remained influential as they retained or regained control of the processing machinery.[161] However, with the formation of ejidos, villages gained access to credit through the Mérida branch of the Banco Nacional de Crédito Ejidal.[162] This led to a reduction in the power of the planter class, although local bosses (including mayors, councilmen, political appointees, leaders of the successive political parties that controlled the government, etc.) stepped into the vacuum, becoming more influential than abstract ideas like ethnicity or class consciousness.[163] By the 1960s, the henequen industry was greatly reduced by foreign competition and the introduction of synthetic fiber sources.[164] However, today items made of henequen fiber such as hats and clothing are still sold in markets throughout Yucatán, aimed at local and tourist audiences.

## CHAPTER 4

# SUGAR AND RUM PRODUCTION ON THE YUCATÁN PENINSULA

SUGAR AND RUM PRODUCTION IN Yucatán were influenced by two major factors: (1) the long growing cycle that affected when and how much labor was needed, and (2) the social relationship between the owner and working class that influenced where sugar was produced. This chapter explores the interrelationship of these factors through a discussion of how sugar growing moved from the central and southeastern portions of the peninsula to the wilds of the northeastern coast. The final section details the authors' work investigating the small site of Xuxub and the larger site of San Eusebio near the northeastern coast of Yucatán.[1]

## THE WILD NORTH COAST OF QUINTANA ROO

The historical trajectory of the northern coast of Quintana Roo, including the Yalahau region, where the authors' ongoing archaeological investigations are focused (see map 2), is quite different from the rest of the Yucatán Peninsula. Within the century following contact, European-introduced diseases resulted in a massive population reduction, perhaps as high as 90 percent. The surviving native peoples were concentrated into settlement regions across the peninsula, but Quintana Roo became a bastion for Maya rebelling against the Spanish.[2] Because of this unstable social environment, in the mid-1500s only six encomiendas were established in Quintana Roo. These were located at the sites of Kantunilkin, Conil, Cozumel, Ecab, Polé, and Zama (Tulum/Tancah).[3]

In 1546, the Maya of what is today Quintana Roo initiated the "Great Revolt" to protest their treatment by the Spanish. Although this uprising was squelched by 1547, the Spanish still regarded the area as hostile.[4] A combination of low population density and little supervision by the Spanish along the northeastern tip of the peninsula fostered the development of piracy in the area.[5] Legends recall pirates hiding their booty along the coast, and by the mid-1600s they began extracting the logwood tree (known locally as *palo de tinte* or *palo tinto*) near Ecab.[6] The Spanish virtually abandoned the region to a small population of Maya and pirates by the mid-1600s because of the difficulty of maintaining the area.[7] This lack of attention continued for the next two centuries, making the region a place of escape for those fed up with the colonial and early postcolonial system.

## INDEPENDENCE, LAND LOSS, AND REVOLUTION

The previous chapter discussed the failure of the elites to live up to their promises of reform and betterment for Indigenous peoples after the war for Mexican independence. The result was loss of land and the Indigenous populations, including Yucatán's Maya, being treated as nothing more than cheap labor instead of full participants in efforts to modernize Yucatán and grow its economy.[8] Haciendas continued to expand, and by 1840, hacienda owners were buying up property, virtually land-locking Maya villages and making it impossible for them to sustain themselves, develop infrastructure, or have access to education.[9]

When the Caste War of the Yucatán Peninsula (Guerra de Castas) started in 1847, the rebels began specifically targeting sugar-producing haciendas for destruction.[10] The war raged on for several years, resulting in massive casualty losses of approximately 40 percent on both sides. By 1850, the armies of Yucatán had secured the western part of the peninsula. The Caste War ended with the defeat of the remaining rebels in most of the Mexican Yucatán by the mid-1850s.[11] The exception was in the southeast, where war raged until finally ending in 1901, when the remaining rebels (the cruceros) were defeated by General Ignacio Bravo and his soldiers.[12] Throughout the conflict, many Maya retreated to the remote "uncontrollable wilds" of the east.[13]

The razing of sugar plantations not only devastated some of the Yucatán's most profitable enterprises, but also led to sugar shortages and curtailed the production of cane alcohol.[14] Those looking to restart production in the 1870s looked to the isolated north coast of Quintana Roo, which had soils suitable for sugarcane. Although the area had once been abandoned to pirates and hostile Maya, the inhabitants of the largest Maya town in the area, known as Kantunilkin, agreed to cease hostilities circa 1855, and instead helped local authorities keep the peace.[15] The region was isolated and lacked infrastructure, but was relatively safe and became the best option for sugar production. This region, which includes our study area, still contains historic ruins of several of these sugar operations.

## SUGAR PRODUCTION IN THE YALAHAU REGION

Since 2009, we have identified four former sugar and rum production sites in the Yalahau region in northern Quintana Roo (see map 2). Two of these sites, known today as Rancho Aznar and Monte Bravo, have scant remaining architecture, as they are both located within actively cultivated farms and have suffered considerable damage. We have identified a third site named Solferino in documents but have never been able to locate it on the ground.[16] Thus, for the sake of this discussion, we will focus on the better-documented and more intact sites of Xuxub and San Eusebio.

### XUXUB

Mauricio Palmero founded the sugar- and rum-producing hacienda known as Xuxub circa 1870 (figure 6, see map 4) and sold it to a U.S.-Mexican partnership of Robert L. Stephens and Ramón Aznar around 1872.[17] Robert L. Stephens, an engineer and adventurer from New Jersey, had come earlier to Yucatán for work. Local businessman Andrés Urcelay had hired him to install machinery at the Solferino sugar mill. Urcelay contracted the boat *Fulita* to transport his expensive equipment from Progreso to Puntachen (see figure 6). The loading of the equipment was delayed one day when no laborers showed up to do the work. The next day, Stephens ordered that the *Fulita* be brought to the dock for loading, but the captain refused, as a storm was coming in and the equipment would take a half day to load. When Stephens persisted and had the boat loaded anyway, the captain left and got drunk. The boat owner found a new captain, who ordered that the boat once again be unloaded. Stephens

**FIGURE 6.** Boat travel through Laguna Yalahau, with Jennifer P. Mathews (front) and local guide (rear). Map of Laguna Yalahau. (Photograph courtesy of Scott L. Fedick; map by John R. Gust.)

refused to allow this, arguing that they should leave soon and avoid the rest of the storm. The captain refused, and that night, the loaded *Fulita* was smashed to pieces against the pier, dumping the equipment into the shallow waters of the port, which required an additional week to salvage. Stephens argued that there would have been no problem had the boat departed, as he originally ordered. However, Andrés Urcelay and his brothers blamed Stephens for damage to the machinery and the resulting delay.[18] This incited an ongoing feud between Stephens and the Urcelays.

Although Stephens lacked capital and knew the pitfalls of working in the area, he saw the promise of sugar production and wanted to purchase an operation of his own. He had operated sugar mills on plantations in Cuba and thus was able to convince Ramón Aznar, a member of a wealthy Mexican family seeking further moneymaking opportunities, to purchase the property of Xuxub.[19] They agreed that Stephens would manage the operation for ten years, after which they would sell the operation and split the profits.[20]

Xuxub, which now sits on Solferino-San Angel ejido land, is located approximately 7.1 km east-southeast of the contemporary town of Chiquila.[21] Today, the only access to Xuxub is by a shallow draft boat through the Laguna Yalahau (see figure 6). Due to its remote location, and probably because he was a white foreigner, Stephens feared an attack by Caste War holdouts, bandits, and contentious neighbors.[22] To make an attack more difficult, he prohibited anyone from cutting a road that would allow access to the operation by land.[23] In spite of this, Balthazar Montilla, a commander of the local National Guard garrison who had been harassing Stephens, ordered a road cut to Xuxub on June 18, 1875.[24]

In April 1875, Bernardino Cen, a former crucero leader, and dozens of rebels loyal to him left the stronghold of Chan Santa Cruz (see map 3).[25] In October 1875, they used Montilla's road to approach and attack Xuxub. Cen and his men pillaged the operation, killing dozens of the workers and Stephens.[26] Upon hearing of the attack, Montilla and his national guardsmen pursued and caught up with Cen's group, who were still hungover from the rum that they looted from Xuxub.[27] Some were captured, but others, including Cen, were killed in the altercation.[28] According to Stephens's aid, Joseph Byrne, and Stephens's widow, Mary, Montilla then destroyed the ledger page that showed the debts that the Urcelay brothers owed to Xuxub.[29] He proceeded to loot barrels of rum, which he then delivered to the home of Andrés Urcelay.[30] This behavior points to some level of collusion between the Urcelays and Montilla, but we do

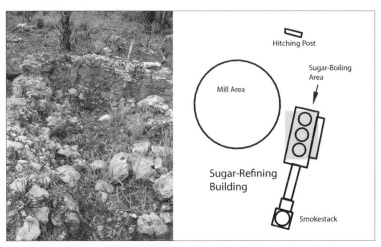

**FIGURE 7.** Sugar-refining building with circular outlines where boiling cauldrons once sat. This area is gray on the accompanying map. (Photograph by Jennifer P. Mathews; map by John R. Gust.)

not know whether Cen simply took advantage of the road Montilla cut, or if Montilla conspired with Cen and then later silenced him.[31]

As Paul Sullivan notes, the documentary history for Xuxub is uneven. Sullivan located an extensive group of archival documents that focus almost entirely on three subjects: (1) Stephens complaining to the United States consulate about local officials harassing him, (2) the investigation into the attack, and (3) the disposition of Xuxub after Stephens's murder.[32] Unfortunately, these documents do not focus on the day-to-day life at Xuxub, which is what most interests the authors as archaeologists. Thus we have had to turn to other sources of information, such as mapping

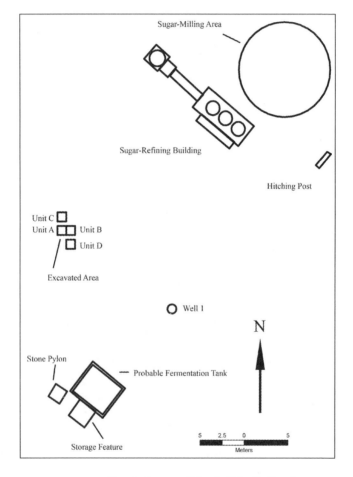

**MAP 4.** Xuxub site core. (Map by John R. Gust.)

**FIGURE 8.** Sugar-milling area at Xuxub. Note the sugar-refining building visible on the left. (Photograph by Jennifer P. Mathews.)

and excavation, artifact analysis, ethnographic interviews, and literature on haciendas elsewhere in Yucatán to attempt to fill in these gaps.

At the ruins of Xuxub (see map 4), we mapped a sugar-refining building with a nearby circular milling area, two wells, a storage feature (a probable fermentation tank), three ancillary post or pylon features, and a low wall that may have acted as a boundary marker or dock.[33] Most of the features are constructed of locally sourced limestone and mortar, although the fire chamber of the smokestack (which was originally approximately 5.5 m tall but was partially destroyed in 2005 by Hurricane Wilma) was lined with heat-resistant brick sourced from the New York City area, based on their brick-maker markings.[34]

At Xuxub and the nearby site of San Eusebio, the sugar-refining buildings were constructed in a style known as a "Jamaica Train," as discussed in chapter 2.[35] The smokestack is connected to a long, linear structure that has rounded interior walls and held three side-by-side kettles (1.0–1.5 m in diameter) for boiling sugarcane juice (figure 7; see map 4). Workers ladled cane juice from cast iron kettle to kettle, as water evaporated, until the juice became a thick syrup. The structure is currently open on top and contains no metal remains, but probably would have had a vegetal superstructure to act as shade, along with some amount of metal piping.

**FIGURE 9.** Fermentation tanks from Xuxub (probable) (left) and Richland Rum (right). (Photographs by John R. Gust.)

Immediately adjacent to this structure, the grinding mill (figure 8) was located in the middle of a low circular structure (11 m in diameter) that was ringed by a single course of stone. The mill was powered by a mule, horse, or person who walked in a circular fashion.[36]

The limestone wall of the probable fermentation tank at Xuxub (figure 9) is lined with limestone-based cement so that it would have been watertight.[37] Although this feature has been identified as a water storage tank, the site has two small wells—one of which is immediately adjacent and still holds water.[38] The necks of both wells are constructed of local stone and mortar, and stand about half a meter tall. The final feature at the site is a single-course wall located adjacent to a natural entrance from the river.[39] The exact function is unknown, but the feature was likely either a boundary wall or the dock where people, supplies, and rum were moved in and out of the site.

Thus far, we have failed to identify the workers' housing at the site, but this may be because the workers lived in structures made of perishable materials, which leave little evidence behind in the archaeological record.[40] Paul Sullivan, who studied the historic documents of Xuxub intensively, believes that approximately thirty families lived and worked on-site.[41] Residence on-site was necessary because Xuxub could not be accessed by land. The site also floods during the sugarcane growing and harvesting season, making much of the land unusable for habitation. We focused our search for worker housing in areas that do not normally flood.

Our fieldwork at Xuxub, conducted between 2009 and 2014, consisted of survey, mapping, surface collection, shovel probes, and limited

**FIGURE 10.** Boundary wall or dock at Xuxub, along with imported ceramics found near the boundary wall or dock feature. (Xuxub photograph by Scott L. Fedick; ceramics photograph by John R. Gust.)

excavation in the habitable areas.[42] Mathews and Gust conducted surface collection in all accessible portions of the site in 2011, and Gust collected artifacts opportunistically during his dissertation fieldwork.[43] The large majority of the assemblage, both in number and by weight, is represented by surface collected artifacts.[44]

Gust excavated shovel probes in the three areas that were large enough to house workers, that were not in the annual flood zone, and either were near freshwater or had artifacts on the surface.[45] These areas included around the wall (figure 10), near the current entrance to the site, around one of the wells, and near the standing structures of the sugar-processing area (see figures 4 and 10–13).[46] In addition to excavating for buried cultural material, Gust collected and tested soil from each shovel probe to determine phosphate concentrations, which are enhanced or degraded by human and animal activity.[47] The phosphate results showed some small anomalies, but these differences did not correlate with other human disturbances of the landscape.[48] Nonetheless, it is likely that at least one of these areas once contained worker housing, simply due to a dearth of other suitable land.[49] The lack of correlation between phosphate levels and artifacts, coupled with the absence of even a single

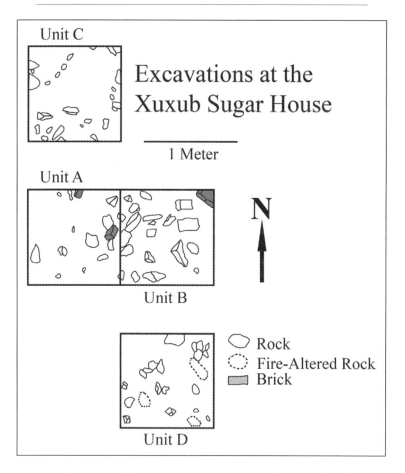

Unit C

Excavations at the
Xuxub Sugar House

1 Meter

Unit A

Unit B

N

Unit D

◯ Rock
◌ Fire-Altered Rock
▨ Brick

**MAP 5.** Locations of Operation 23 excavation units, bottom of Level 1. Note the fire-altered rock in unit D. (Map by John R. Gust.)

course of stone house foundations, likely imply that the workers were living simply and not performing activities that left a lasting mark on the landscape.[50]

One shovel probe yielded clay floor tiles possibly consistent with those Sullivan reports to have been present in Stephens's house. Gust excavated four 1 m by 1 m excavation units to further investigate clay floor tile fragments found within a shovel probe near the standing structures.[51] Along with brick and additional clay tile, these excavations contained a concentration of ashy soil and the remains of three burned limestone rocks arranged in an equilateral triangle (see figure 9). If Maya women were cooking meals in a kitchen area near Stephens's home, we might interpret this as a three-stone hearth. However, the stones are farther apart than we would expect for a three-stone hearth, hinting at the possibility that these stones may have been the points where the rum was still anchored (map 5). If so, the tile was from the distillery building, not a home. It would also mean that all major facilities for sugar production and rum distillation—the sugarcane mill, water source, sugar-refining building, fermentation tank, and distillery—were located in one small area (see map 4).

The artifact assemblage that we collected from Xuxub reflects the residents' way of life and their connection to the global economy. Surface artifacts were concentrated between the standing structures and east-northeast of the site, along an intermittent watercourse.[52] The first of these were likely a focal point of site activity, although those along the watercourse were likely placed there during intermittent flooding. We flagged the last location along the boundary wall or dock as the probable point of ingress to the site. The imported ceramics (see figure 10) and bottle glass found there indicated it was also a possible site for worker housing, although the phosphorus analysis did not add support for this interpretation.[53]

When looking at the site as a whole, the international nature of the assemblage is apparent. We found bottles from México, Martinique, and the United States, as well as one embossed in Portuguese at the site, and we believe that most were brought to México on ships from the United States.[54] We recovered one complete (figure 11) and one partial Murray and Lanman's Florida Water bottle that originated in New York, both of which were embossed in Spanish, implying that they were produced specifically for the Latin American market. Florida Water is a lightly scented cologne that Lanman & Kemp Barclay, the successor company to Murray and Lanman's, still markets as a cure-all for minor topical maladies like nonvenomous bug bites and itchy scalp.[55] We also found an olive-green square bottle fragment with a molded base that has a raised inscription for Udolp'ho Wolfe's Scheidam Aromatic Schnapps.[56] This product was marketed as a "patent medicine" used for curing colds, but also may have been misused as an intoxicant. We recovered three partial milk-glass screw-top jars in the clearing near the sugarhouse. The jars' bases include the embossed lettering of "MENTH . . ." and "TRADE MARK." Although no paper label remains on the body, the pieces are

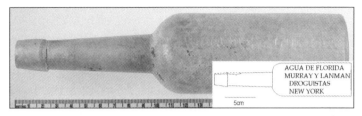

AGUA DE FLORIDA
MURRAY Y LANMAN
DROGUISTAS
NEW YORK

5cm

**FIGURE 11.** Murray and Lanman's Florida Water bottle. (Photograph and drawing by John R Gust.)

**FIGURE 12.** Rhum Negrita bottle found at Xuxub. (Photograph by Jennifer P. Mathews.)

**FIGURE 13.** Terra cotta vessel handle (left) and neck of a large olla jar (right), both found at Xuxub. (Photographs by John R. Gust.)

**FIGURE 14.** Green transfer print bowl depicting a classical scene. (Photograph by John R. Gust.)

most similar to jars made by the Mentholatum Company of Buffalo, New York. We recovered a Scott's Emulsion Cod Liver Oil medicine bottle that likely dates to somewhere between the 1870s and 1890s.[57] Not surprisingly, we found several large olive-green "demijohn" fragments from hand-blown glass vessels that were likely used for storing rum. Lastly, the bottle from Martinique (figure 12) is from high-quality rum, rhum agricole, made by the Bardinet Company, and likely brought in after the site ceased production.[58]

We retrieved the closures (or finishes) of thirty-two bottles, seventeen of which were the crown-cap type that was not introduced until 1892.[59] The other two datable finishes are similar to finishes that were not introduced until 1895.[60] Thus, of the seventeen to nineteen datable finishes found, none were produced before 1892, which is seventeen years after the site was attacked.[61] This would indicate a continued occupation or reoccupation of the site after the massacre, but does not clarify who was living there.

Expectedly, building material and hardware collectively made up more than a fifth of the artifact assemblage that we recovered. Some of these items were nails and discarded machetes, but we also found a brick made in New Jersey, along with "French" style or interlocking style red clay roof tiles that we think may have come from the Mound City Roofing Tile Company, based in St. Louis, Missouri.[62] Only the manager may have lived in a house with a clay floor and roof tiles, although these could also have been part of the distillery structure.[63]

Xuxub yielded a number of different patterns of imported ceramic tableware, or "china." In most cases, all that we recovered was a small piece or two of the vessels. The finds include a small piece of a vessel with flow-blue design that almost perfectly frames a small pagoda, a large orange-brown terra-cotta vessel handle, the neck of a large olla (figure 13), a bowl with blue stripes, a plain pedestal bowl, a fragment of an incised green bowl, two blue-and-purple transfer print patterns, and a bowl with a painted flower pattern. The most complete vessel we recovered is a green, transfer print, steep-side bowl with a classical design featuring an urn and cherub (figure 14).

The paucity of the faunal assemblage suggests that the people at Xuxub, although located on the coast, were not consuming the cockle and conch that people at San Eusebio were catching.[64] However, small fish are also available nearby, and their absence in the faunal assemblage may be an issue of poor preservation rather than lack of exploitation. As at the neighboring site of San Eusebio, the lack of groundstone artifacts and few locally produced ceramics is puzzling, particularly as significant quantities of groundstone were found at the contemporaneous Maya site of San Pedro Siris in western Belize.[65] Nonetheless, we did find the remains of metal, hand-crank corn grinders at Xuxub and San Eusebio, imported from the United States.[66]

Xuxub is a contradiction, as it was made purposefully difficult to reach and yet it contains a wide variety of luxury goods from outside of México. This variety of artifacts defies the categorization by material type that archaeologists usually present. Using a typology that is based on function, it is easier to reconstruct past activities of the site's inhabitants, as artifacts of a single material may have multiple functions, or artifacts of multiple materials may be used to complete a single function.[67]

Alcohol bottles represent the largest portion of the artifact assemblage by weight (29.6 percent), but this is misleading, as, due to their late date of manufacture, these items either date late in Xuxub's operation as a sugar- and rum-production center or postdate it altogether. One possibility is that Stephens controlled the number of bottles at the site to limit pilferage of the rum produced there. Thus the lack of alcohol bottles dating to the rum-making period is not indicative of actual alcohol consumption.

Building materials, including bricks, roofing, and floor tiles, represent 20.7 percent of the total assemblage and were concentrated near the sugarhouse and surrounding structures. All recovered building materials are associated with the operation of Xuxub and possibly Stephens's house. No building material has been recovered from worker housing.

Personal-use items, including perfume, cosmetic containers, and medicine bottles, make up 18.2 percent of the assemblage. Much of this consists of the Florida Water bottles, marketed both as a perfume and remedy for insect bites. This latter use makes sense at Xuxub, where mosquitoes are a constant annoyance. Subsistence-related artifacts make up 16.5 percent of the artifacts that we recovered from the site. This seems like a small amount of the assemblage for a group of residential workers and their families. Most of this is equipment for preparing food, but plates and bowls represent only 3.9 percent of the site assemblage.[68] What the residents were eating off of is still a mystery, as locally produced ceramics comprise only 3.2 percent of the assemblage total, and much of this is from the neck of a single large water-storage jar. Inhabitants would not have taken broken ceramic tableware during abandonment, but they would have removed durable metal cooking pots. Hardware, including

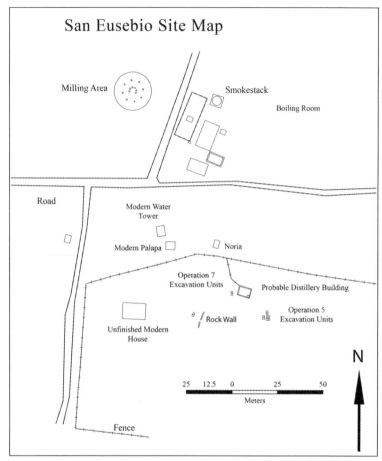

**MAP 6.** San Eusebio site. (Map by John R. Gust.)

tools, represent 4.5 percent of the total site assemblage. This is mostly fasteners and metal wire, with some heavily rusted machete fragments as well. These artifacts were also centered near the sugar works.

## SAN EUSEBIO

Southwest of Xuxub lies the site of San Eusebio. In 1876, La Compania Agricola del Cuyo y Anexas (El Cuyo) was given a 1,800 square kilometer land grant along the northeast coast of the Yucatán Peninsula.[69] This grant was part of a program instituted by the administration of President

Porfirio Díaz. They wished to cement the peace in the area by bringing in companies to develop jobs and infrastructure.[70] They gave another grant of 2,410.83 square kilometers to El Cuyo's competitor and eventual purchaser, La Compania Colonizadora de la Costa Oriente de Yucatán.[71] El Cuyo established several jobs sites, or fincas, in the region, and produced or extracted materials including honey, wax, dyewood, and salt. At San Eusebio (map 6) the El Cuyo company produced sugar, which was ultimately sold as refined sugar, sugar cubes, and rum.[72]

The major architectural components of the site are a smokestack, the cane-grinding area, a subterranean tank, three to four freshwater features, a small industrial building, and the remains of a small house or office. The smokestack at San Eusebio is significantly larger than at Xuxub (figure 15) and still standing.[73] This structure is made with high-quality local stone and mortar, well-suited to the application. Just south of the smokestack sits the Jamaica Train sugar-processing house.[74] There is a tunnel running underneath the sugar-processing building that may have been used for storage, although the current state of the building makes further interpretation difficult.

The milling area and subterranean tank are located west of the smokestack and adjacent to the south end of the processing building, respectively. The circular milling area today is cut approximately 1 m into the ground and includes fourteen concrete and stone pylons that likely acted as the base for the sugarcane grinder and a raised floor. The subterranean feature was possibly the fermentation tank, as it would have kept the fermenting liquid at a consistent temperature.[75] Although it could have held freshwater or been used to store cut cane, these explanations seem unlikely due to there being other water-associated features, including three large improved wells, known as *norias* in various states of ruin.[76] The tank is also too small to accommodate storing considerable amounts of cane. Either of these other functions would also mean that there was not a fermentation tank at the site.[77]

A small industrial building in the southeast portion of the site appears to be a storehouse, the company store, a distillery, or it may have acted as all of these. It is built of stone and mortar and has a triangular roof line, indicating there was once a pitched roof, though none of the roof material remains (figure 16). The walls of the structure currently contain two openings in addition to the doorway. The first is a small circular hole located in the back wall.[78] This appears to have once held a stovepipe that could have acted as a vent for a still, but no such machinery is in place

**FIGURE 15.** Smokestack at San Eusebio. (Copyright Macduff Everton 2019, image 35093.)

**FIGURE 16.** Front view of industrial building at San Eusebio (left). Shaft in back corner of building to cellar (right). (Front-view photograph copyright Macduff Everton 2019, image 35096; shaft photograph by John R. Gust.)

today. The second opening may have been a small window but appears more likely to be a result of wall collapse. The doorway is large and once had stout, wooden double doors, as are seen throughout the Yucatán Peninsula.[79] An opening in the southeast corner of the floor leads to a cellar.[80] The cellar is approximately 2 m tall and seems to extend below most, if not all, of the ground floor, although we have not explored it due to safety concerns. The lack of windows indicate that this building was constructed to be secure at the expense of any relative comfort for those working inside. Finally, the damaged remains of a small structure that, according to local residents, once had stone, half-story walls sits on a slight natural rise west-southwest of the industrial building.[81] Locals believe this feature is the remains of a site manager's home or office.

Some of the best information for the operation and conditions at San Eusebio comes from melding the archaeological and documentary data.[82] Gust recovered a fairly complete set of labor records for San Eusebio for thirty-two weeks covering 1909–10 from the *Ramo de Justicia* collection at the General Archives of the State of Yucatán, in Mérida, Yucatán.[83] These records indicate the presence of company stores at both San Eusebio and the El Cuyo company's main operation located at the town of El Cuyo, Yucatán. Most operations elsewhere in the Yucatán Peninsula paid in company scrip instead of cash. We have not found scrip for Xuxub or San Eusebio, but we do know of hacienda tokens for Cuyo de Ancona (figure 17), the company that was reorganized to become El Cuyo.[84] There is no reason to believe that El Cuyo would have changed to paying workers in cash, and the presence of a company store at San Eusebio reinforces this notion.[85]

These labor records offer a point of comparison to haciendas elsewhere in the Yucatán Peninsula. As discussed in chapter 2, there are three broad types of workers: (1) salaried managers; (2) salarios (salaried laborers), who were paid at daily or weekly rates; and (3) jornaleros (piece-rate laborers), who were paid at day and piece rates. Generally, all working-class laborers started as piece-rate workers. White and Mestizo laborers started as piece-rate workers and were often promoted to salaried status over time, but Maya workers were less likely to be promoted.[86]

Management does not appear on the 1909–10 pay records, and thus it is difficult to discern the specific roles played by managers. Salaried laborers included the *mecanico*,[87] who oversaw the sugar works; *plataformeros*, who operated the mule-drawn Decauville narrow-gauge railways (figure 18); *caladores* (boil men), who tended the sugar cauldrons; and the distiller. Piece-rate workers most often were responsible for a task tied to an area, or for cutting a prescribed number of pieces of wood or cane. For example, a worker would be assigned to weed a 20 m by 20 m area,[88] or to cut and dress 300 stalks of sugarcane. Salarios were paid 12.7 percent more per week on average than jornaleros (5.24 pesos compared to 4.65 pesos), but this number most likely underreports the true difference, as wives and children of jornaleros elsewhere were sometimes expected to help, but only the jornalero appears on the labor rolls.[89] Thus this 4.65 pesos per week for jornaleros includes labor performed by unnamed others as well.

The 1909–10 labor records indicate a breakdown of the salario/jornalero dichotomy. Holders of a few positions, most notably the mecanicos, only appear on the labor rolls as salaried workers. Most other workers who labored at day rates also worked at piece rates at some point. The change back and forth between these statuses from week to week, or sometimes within a single week, indicates that this was not simply jornaleros being promoted. The true separation appears to be based on whether workers were temporary or permanent. A small minority of workers appear on the majority of the weekly labor records, and almost two-thirds appear on records for four or fewer weeks (appendix, table 1).

**FIGURE 17.** Five centavos hacienda token from Cuyo de Ancona, precursor company to La Compania Agricola del Cuyo y Anexas, the owner of San Eusebio. (Photograph by John R. Gust.)

**FIGURE 18.** Chicleros (natural chewing-gum base collectors) and their families sitting on a Decauville railcar, near Puerto Morelos, Quintana Roo. Small (12 cm) railroad spike found at San Eusebio. (Chicleros photograph courtesy of Jorge Sánchez; spike photograph by John R. Gust.)

A final group of workers are found only in the receipts paid to labor contractors. It is unknown who these workers were, but they were likely immigrants. The receipts were signed in Chinese (see figure 2) and Korean and included a small premium (usually 6.25 percent) over the wages of named workers. As discussed in chapter 3, it was common for hacienda owners elsewhere on the peninsula to refuse to loan money to immigrants, as owners feared that rootless people could just leave.[90] The additional 6.25 percent may be the labor contractor's fee, a small additional amount paid to make up for the lack of access to the perks of the paternalistic debt peonage system, or both. Maya male laborers were often treated poorly, but even they were not nameless.[91]

The separation of temporary versus permanent workers in the paperwork may indicate a more general shift from the paternalism of debt peonage to a free-labor system. Previously workers were abused, but they were not disposable. Regardless, contemporary residents in the hamlet of San Eusebio told Paul Sullivan that they believed that workers at San Eusebio were debt peons and that the "slaves" were freed when the revolution arrived.[92]

Finally, the labor records illuminate some of the details surrounding the San Eusebio operation. Records indicate that there was regular contact between the operations at San Eusebio and Solferino.[93] National

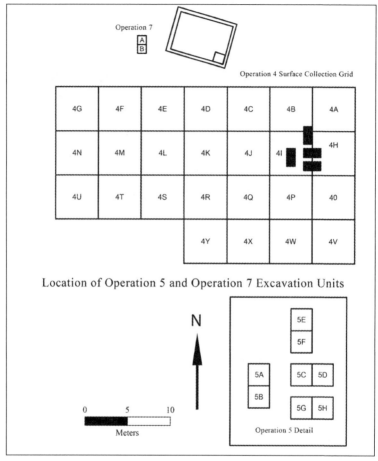

**MAP 7.** Location of the Operation 4 surface collection grid, and Operations 5 and 7 excavation units. (Map by John R. Gust.)

Oceanic and Atmospheric Administration storm track and intensity records indicate that the northern Yucatán Peninsula was hit by a tropical storm on August 6, 1909, and that the peninsula was hit by a hurricane a few weeks later on August 26.[94] The response to these storms provides some additional details about the operations of San Eusebio. Workers were paid to repair telephone lines and reconstruct homes in the weeks following these storms. Telephone service at such a remote location is an indication of its status as a cutting-edge operation.

Fieldwork at San Eusebio consisted of excavation of shovel probes spread out across the site, limited excavation at the southeast portion of the site near the industrial building, and systematic and opportunistic surface collections.[95] The shovel probes were used to investigate areas of the site near standing structures in the hopes of identifying trash pits, activity areas, and worker housing. The operation of a sugar mill requires space for activities like storing firewood, stacking cut sugarcane prior to extraction of the cane juice, and staging the crushed cane for burning or disposal afterward. Gust collected soil samples from shovel probes for phosphate testing, as at Xuxub, with similarly frustrating results.[96] As expected, when using prospecting methods, few shovel probes contained artifacts. When Gust recovered artifacts, they generally came from near the industrial building. He found a large scatter of mostly glass artifacts on the surface west-southwest of the building, and placed excavation units south of the building and near its doorway on the west side (map 7).

The artifacts that Gust recovered from the doorway excavation units lend credence to the interpretation that the building was a storehouse or company store.[97] Many of the artifacts were metal and included hardware fasteners (screws, nuts, bolts, and nails), wire, a short section of chain, two rifle shells and one bullet (all .22 caliber), a small buckle for shoes or a belt, worn machetes, and metal files. He found a few small pieces of local and imported ceramics in these units, all undecorated except for one piece that was yellow on the eating surface with a black line on the other side. None of the ceramics were big enough to determine what kind of vessel they came from. He did find a small green candy jar lid (figure 19) and a Lea and Perrins Worcestershire sauce bottle stopper (figure 20), along with small bottle glass fragments.

Excavations at the south side of the industrial building yielded much of the same material as found elsewhere on-site, including metal fasteners and bottle glass in colors that usually indicate both alcoholic and nonalcoholic contents.[98] There were four interesting finds in these units. The first was two small, decorative, brass finials. The second find was two small pieces of kaolin (clay mineral) tobacco pipes, similar to pipes found at the contemporaneous Maya site of San Pedro Siris in Belize.[99] The third find is a small railroad spike (see figure 18), which is the only recovered artifact from the narrow-gauge Decauville railways that operated at the site. The fourth interesting find is a concentration of cockle and small conch shells that were either discarded food remains or the

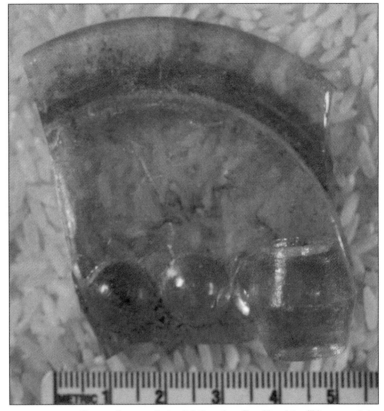

**FIGURE 19.** Green glass candy jar lid found at San Eusebio. (Photograph by John R. Gust.)

remnants of paving material. As the shore is more than 3 km away, marine animals were probably collected as food, and then the shells were reused or discarded.

Almost half of the artifacts by weight were collected from a 625 m² area, south of the distillery / company store / storehouse building.[100] The artifacts are primarily large beverage-style bottles and bottle fragments of varying colors that provide a clue to probable contents.[101] Bottles that are amber (brown), green, olive green, and black usually contained alcoholic beverages. Brown glass generally designated beer or liquor, while green, black, and olive glass bottles tended to contain wine and sometimes liquor.[102] Most bottles that are aqua-colored today were clear when in use and contained Florida Water or nonalcoholic beverages like mineral

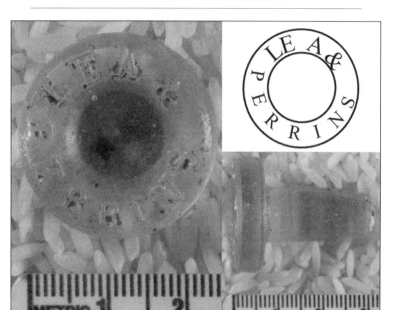

**FIGURE 20.** Lea and Perrins Worcestershire sauce stopper. (Photographs and drawing by John R. Gust.)

water.[103] Other artifacts include two bottles from perfume or patent medicine, and two bottles from Bálsamo del Dr. Castro (Dr. Castro's Balm), a claimed cure-all for everything from head and muscle aches to abdominal pain and mosquito bites (figure 21).[104]

The improved white earthenware ceramics from this area are generally small fragments and more than three quarters are undecorated. Those that are decorated are a mix of painted, striped, and transfer print wares in blue, brown, red, and green. Only one piece was large enough to identify it as coming from the base of a pedestal bowl. There were also small pieces of stoneware and porcelain. Like Xuxub, the imported ceramics from San Eusebio are interesting because the breadth of style, color, and type of decoration demonstrate the access that this remote population had to worldwide markets. There is everything from painted floral patterns to simple striped designs, and transfer print in a number of colors but in smaller quantities than would be expected for a residential site.

Other artifacts from this surface collection area include metal fasteners of various types, strap metal, a corn-grinding wheel, brick fragments, a two-handed mano (the only groundstone recovered from the site), and

**FIGURE 21.** Bálsamo del Dr. Castro bottle found at San Eusebio. (Photograph and drawing by John R. Gust.)

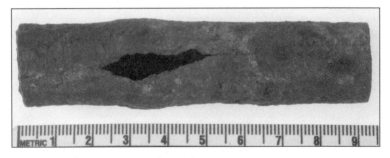

**FIGURE 22.** Small section of burst copper pipe found near the industrial building at San Eusebio. (Photograph by John R. Gust.)

a small section of metal pipe that burst under pressure (figure 22). The proximity of the pipe to the industrial building bolsters the idea that it was used as the distillery.

Interpretatively this site is enigmatic, and unfortunately, the soil phosphate analysis and shovel probes did not help define production activity areas or housing. Comparison of artifact frequencies by function (appendix, tables 2 and 3) supports the idea that few workers were living at San Eusebio, as subsistence-related artifacts comprise more than two and a half times more of the assemblage, by percentage, at Xuxub than at San Eusebio.[105] This is not surprising, as San Eusebio, unlike Xuxub, is accessible by land. That almost twice as much hardware (by percentage of the total assemblage) was found at San Eusebio compared with Xuxub may reflect that San Eusebio's better capitalization resulted in a better stock of supplies for repairs.[106]

Bottle glass represents more than half of all the cultural material recovered from the site by weight.[107] Unlike at Xuxub, alcohol bottles represent less of the assemblage than bottles from personal use items like Florida Water, mineral water, medicine, and cosmetics. There are many domestic artifacts on-site that would normally point to households, but as mentioned previously, a company store is known to have operated at San Eusebio and would have also supplied those goods.[108] Much of the bottle glass was concentrated in a scatter near the industrial building. If this feature was not created through on-site domestic use and breakage, then what could account for the large artifact scatter with so much bottle glass? Although hypothetical, one explanation is that only a few workers lived at San Eusebio (fitting the residency pattern for sugar workers elsewhere in the Yucatán Peninsula; see chapter 2) and the industrial building was the company store. Another hypothesis is that when the Mexican Revolution reached San Eusebio, the workers attacked the company store that had oppressed them, raided its stock, and destroyed it.

## CONCLUSIONS

The history of rum and sugar production in the Yucatán Peninsula reflects the inherent harshness of the sugar business. Internal politics of the peninsula resulted in the north coast, which was once nearly abandoned by the Spanish because it was too wild, suddenly being considered desirable because of its suitable soils and location outside of the area where the Caste War still simmered.[109] Land seizures and oppressive employment systems, including debt peonage and the forced use of company stores through payment in scrip, were necessary to coerce the resistant labor force to work in the sugarcane fields.

Unlike other sugar-producing regions, most production in the Yucatán Peninsula was not for export, but to meet local demand for sugar and cane alcohol. Rum from operations like San Eusebio and Xuxub was sold in the cantinas of Yucatecan cities and towns (see chapter 5) and remained a mainstay of company stores throughout the peninsula.[110] However, despite their remote location and their limited local distribution of their product, we find surprisingly cosmopolitan objects such as U.S.-imported bricks, tile, corn grinders, cologne, decorated dishes, and medicine, indicating that they were tied to international trade markets.

One mystery that remains regarding the artifacts of the sugar and rum production sites in northern Quintana Roo is why so little of the metal equipment is found on these sites compared with similarly aged sugar-related sites in Belize. Our best explanation is that sites were mined for scrap metal during particularly bad economic times in the region. An intriguing alternative hypothesis is that in response to General Salvador Alvarado's Dry Law, stills were moved to secluded locations so that legal sugar could be produced in the open while illegal rum was produced in hidden locations.[111] Today, economic activity in northern Quintana Roo is focused around tourism. The development and continuing growth of the Cancun region is the subject of chapter 5.

# CHAPTER 5

# THE CANTINA, THE STATE, AND THE DEVELOPMENT OF CANCÚN

THE RELATIONSHIP BETWEEN ALCOHOL AND the state cannot be overstated, nor can the relationship between alcohol and the economy of Yucatán. The state has long regulated the manufacture and sale of alcoholic products and continues to do so today. Colonial authorities had incentive to blunt or redirect the worst effects of citizens' overindulgence of alcohol and, as they were also often hacienda owners themselves, to reinforce stereotypes that portrayed Indigenous peoples as in need of their paternalistic guiding hand. Rum and other alcohol thus played an integral role in the creation of Yucatán's wealth and contributed to ongoing social inequality. European and European-descended elites built upon and manipulated existing Maya social mores around alcohol manufacture, sale, and consumption. Yet, for the frustrated worker, drinking was a temporary escape that often mired him and his family in further debt, compelling the family to continue their life on the hacienda.[1]

The postcontact history of the eastern coast of Yucatán is different than that of the other side of the peninsula. It is a history of boom and bust, a history of people trying and failing to profit from mahogany and chicle extraction, cattle farming, and sugar and rum production, among other products. Rum is one product that bridges Yucatán's past and present, as it was once as intrinsic to the henequen economy in the west as it is now to the tourist economy in the east along the "Maya Riviera."

Cancun is a city designed around the tourist, and unlike the Mérida area, Cancun is decidedly ahistorical. The grittiness of downtown is screened off from its visitors who stay primarily in the *Zona Hotelera*. It is the place for the visitor to escape their lives for a little while, and not have to think about the struggles of others. Cancun is also a city built on rum, where rum drinks flow freely.

This chapter investigates the ways in which the sale, use, and abuse of rum are the predicates for Yucatán today. It begins by briefly examining precontact alcohol and then looks at the development of distilled alcohol in México. It notes that the popularity of this more potent alcohol contributed to the growth of the Mérida cantina. Further, this chapter looks at the ways that women, both poor and elite, used the cantina (and bars more generally) to carve out an existence in a society in which they had little place except as wives and mothers. We will also examine how reforms following the Méxican Revolution stripped cantina women of their financial well-being in the name of protecting morality. Finally, we explore the comparison between the rum-fueled cantinas of nineteenth-century Mérida with the alcohol-driven tourism in the east during the twentieth century. Although the cantina in Mérida and the bars and clubs in Cancun are quite different settings, both were adapted by, if not constructed through, state practice.

## ALCOHOL IN PRECONTACT MESOAMERICA

The importance of alcoholic drink in Mesoamerican ritual is depicted in precontact iconography and demonstrated with the Yucatec and Lacandon Maya use of balché during the twentieth century.[2] Alcohol in pre-Hispanic México is the subject of several book-length works, including those by Henry J. Bruman, Alfonso Paredes, Tim Mitchell, and a multi-author volume edited by Gretchen Pierce and Áurea Toxqui.[3] Drawing on these works as a baseline, our contribution is to focus on the specific effects of European conquest on issues concerning the Maya and the use of alcohol in the nineteenth century. Prior to European contact, there is little evidence that Mesoamericans used distillation techniques.[4] Various cultures consumed alcoholic drinks throughout México and the rest of Latin America prior to European contact, although the kinds of drinks varied by region. As Bruman notes, the Maya region had a long and varied history of alcoholic beverages derived from sources, including corn,

**FIGURE 23.** Aztec pulque ritual performed on two rabbits. (*Florentine Codex*, book 4, chapters 4 and 5.)

**FIGURE 24.** Aztec pulque ritual. (*Codex Magliabechiano*, 85r.)

agave, pineapple, jocote, coyol palm, and the balché tree.[5] While Indigenous alcoholic beverages sometimes had psychotropic effects, the alcohol content was similar to that of beer or wine, and thus did not have the potency of distilled spirits.[6]

Pulque (*octli*) is a weak alcoholic drink made of the fermented juice of a few varieties of agave,[7] with an alcohol content similar to modern beer. Consumption of pulque was initially restricted to ritual feasts and religious rites (figures 23 and 24),[8] although pregnant and nursing women (figure 25) and the elderly (male and female) were allowed to drink it daily. For the Aztecs, the sale of pulque and public drunkenness was a capital offense. The first time an elite was caught intoxicated in public, or the second incident for someone from the lower classes, resulted in a death sentence.[9]

Balché is made by soaking the bark of the balché tree (*Lonchocarpus violaceus*) in honey and water and allowing it to ferment.[10] The brewing of balché rotated between the respected men of a community, and they

**FIGURE 25.** Aztec goddess Mayahual depicted as a maguey (agave) plant, breastfeeding an infant. (*Codex Fejérváry-Mayer*, 28.)

only imbibed the drink during ritual ceremonies.[11] Chuchiak reports that after European contact, rules were relaxed to allow prominent women to attend the rituals as well. Like many traditions, the balché ceremonies had both sacred and mundane functions. The religious component was used to continue Maya belief systems, which were in opposition to Roman Catholicism. Ritual imbibing was a central component in *cofradia* ceremonies, and those who did not consume could not participate as brothers (*cofrades*) or community elders.[12] The strengthening of internal community bonds acted to cement solidarity and stirred up resistance to Spanish demands. The Spanish viewed these ceremonies as civil violations and religious transgressions for idolatry, and thus both secular and religious authorities handled the prosecutions for balché production and consumption. They would arrest those caught participating in the balché ceremonies, driving the ceremonies underground. To further undermine the ceremonies, the Spanish attempted to kill all the balché trees, which led Maya to hide and protect the trees.[13] Balché use persisted into the twentieth century, as Redfield and Villa Rojas discussed balché throughout their study of the postrevolutionary town Chan Kom. Unlike many other towns in postrevolutionary Yucatán, Chan Kom served balché and aguardiente rum at celebrations and used them ritually, although balché was preferred.[14]

Ancient peoples also produced corn beer, best known by its Peruvian name, chicha, virtually anywhere that corn was grown.[15] While women in México have overseen chicha production since pre-Hispanic times, relatively little is known about the mores surrounding its use prior to contact. After European Contact, sugar became part of the base of Maya maize chicha. Observers noted that Indigenous peoples preferred sugar-based alcoholic beverages, and by the latter part of the colonial period, aguardiente began to supplement and then displace the use of chicha by Maya and the population as a whole.[16]

## ALCOHOL IN MESOAMERICA FROM THE COLONIAL PERIOD TO THE MEXICAN REVOLUTION

Following conquest, some religious officials still exhibited concerns regarding alcohol consumption. As Bristol notes, "In the 1540s the friar Toribio de Benavente, also known as Motolinfa, condemned pulque for making Indigenous people 'violently drunk and accordingly more cruel and bestial' while acknowledging that 'actually, if taken with moderation, [pulque] is wholesome and very nutritious.'"[17] There were also governmental misgivings about pulque bars, known as *pulquerias*, although laws regulating pulque were relaxed and elites provided pulque to participants in communal labor.[18] Once pulque became an important trade item, the control of production wound up in the hands of men. Women, however, did continue to run the majority of the estimated 850 clandestine pulquerias on the outskirts of México City. Even legal (licensed) establishments poured illegally made or smuggled alcohol.[19]

European-introduced aguardiente, a crude rum made from sugarcane, differed from pulque in its strength and the fact that it could be procured and consumed outside of the festive environment of the pulqueria.[20] People often consumed outside of the regulating influence of social networks. As Carey states, "As a commodity that was produced and consumed locally (and often illicitly), aguardiente (distilled sugarcane liquor or rum) was frequently at the center of economic, political, and social conflicts within and between local communities and between communities and the state."[21]

## LIQUOR, RACE, AND INDIGENOUS CULTURE

For centuries, alcohol was a key component of community and family rituals, and continued to be an integral part of maintaining cultural identity after the conquest. For example, in Guatemala, some Maya avoided the legal ramifications of smuggling alcohol by insisting that it was for use in traditional ritual and customs.[22] This exception was later expanded to include Roman Catholic and Maya holidays, as well as secular rituals like the changing of town leadership.[23] Among the Zinancanteco Maya of Chiapas, when a mayordomo was leaving office, he hosted a formal meal with chicken and rum for the incoming mayordomo and shamans. They concluded the feast with a ritual circuit in which rum, candles, and incense were offered to the Earth Lord.[24] The Zinancanteco also gifted bottles of rum to shamans for curing rituals and to midwives around the sixth or seventh month of pregnancy (to secure their services). Following the birth of an infant, they served three rounds of rum to the family.[25]

During the Hacienda Period in Yucatán, rum was an integral part of the marriage process. Guests expected the families of the bride and groom, or the bride and groom themselves, to provide them with abundant food and drink during the marriage ceremony. This was still expected during Zinancanteco courtship and marriage in the twentieth century. Once a boy selected a girl to marry, he approached his parents with a bottle of rum. If they chose to accept it, they agreed to help him with courtship expenses and to ask the girl to marry him. If his father disapproved of his choice, he refused the bottle of rum. Similarly, the girl's parents showed approval of the marriage by their acceptance of four special bottles of rum presented by the boy's father. Appointed drink pourers arrived at the girl's house and presented the four bottles at the father's feet and requested his permission. The drink pourers distributed the rum during a long ceremony in which petitioners tried to persuade the parents. Throughout the night the parents refused the offer of rum, until the father finally succumbed and took a drink, symbolically giving his daughter away and formally initiating the courtship process. The boy was then summoned from his home, and he arrived carrying serving glasses and a liter of rum. He then served his future father-in-law and relatives until everyone was drunk, and after his petitioners departed, he helped his prospective parents-in-law to bed and gave them more rum if they awoke during the night and in the morning to alleviate their hangovers.[26] Rum was served to the wedding party (minus the bride and groom) immediately following the marriage ceremony outside the church, during the procession from the church back to the bride and groom's new home, as well as upon their arrival. A server provided drinks during a dancing ceremony, which continued until virtually everyone was drunk.[27] Rum was also served at Zinancanteco funerals, baptisms, confirmations, year renewal ceremonies, and cargo ceremonies.[28]

Despite this ready adoption of distilled alcohol into traditional rituals, state officials viewed the introduction of liquor as having a negative effect on many native peoples, leading to the unfortunate stereotype of the "drunkard Indian" in the Americas. White elites claimed that alcohol, and the perceived inability to responsibly use it, was a mark of Indigenous inferiority in early-twentieth-century Guatemala.[29] As one Guatemalan intellectual stated, "The bottle of aguardiente is his consolation, his happiness, the rude companion of his life. The Indian learns to drink since his childhood and to that can be attributed a great part of his degeneration."[30] However, as discussed in chapter 2, some landowners gave rum to young children to get them hooked on it as a way to indebt them, to keep a pliable workforce, and of course the hacienda stores were the principal sellers of rum to workers.[31] Through a form of structural violence, landowners intentionally placed children and workers in harm's way to benefit themselves, and they were encouraged to "compulsively consume."[32] Thus, under this structure of social inequality, the compulsion for drinking alcohol outside of a ritual context came to exist along with ritual drinking in Maya communities.[33] The racist assumption of a generalized genetic predisposition to alcoholism or a cultural inability to regulate consumption came to be a part of physical and social character of the "Indian." In reality, Europeans and Mestizos had their own struggles with liquor, and arrest records from early-twentieth-century Guatemala show that authorities arrested Mestizos for public intoxication at a rate nearly twice that of Indigenous Maya people.[34]

Current research demonstrates that social ills like poverty, lack of opportunity, and lack of control over one's life are greater indicators of the likelihood of systemic alcohol abuse than genetics. Widespread alcoholism in impoverished areas is a result of short-term escapes from the frustrations of life, eventually developing into dependency. Thus it was Europeans who not only introduced liquor but destroyed existing mores around alcohol consumption, while also imposing the very conditions from which many enslaved or colonized people around the world sought a respite.[35]

## LIQUOR, HACENDADOS, AND THE DEBT PEON

As discussed in chapter 2, although members of the elite in Yucatecan society complained about Maya workers engaging in drunkenness, neither the laws nor the practices on the haciendas discouraged this behavior. Spanish (and then Mexican) law stated that people were in essence not fully culpable for acts that they committed while drunk, thus encouraging the appearance of being inebriated or being in an inebriated state.[36] Hacienda owners usually paid their workers in company scrip that was only accepted at the company store, where aguardiente was widely available at inflated prices.[37] Attachment to the hacienda by debt obligations effectively made the debt peon and their families wards of the hacendado.[38] Hacendados may have felt that it was not in their financial interest to restrict worker access to aguardiente, as they failed to take steps to limit the supply.

Thus we see the laws regarding alcohol consumption appear to help elites acquire a stable workforce and diffuse collective action. Hacendados sometimes served as lawmakers and ran in powerful social circles. Had they felt the need to do something about alcohol use on the haciendas, they had the power to do so. The fact that they did not is important to understanding the place of alcohol—in particular, the preferred alcohol of the working class, aguardiente—in the maintenance of nineteenth- and early twentieth-century Yucatecan society.

## FROM SACRED SPACES TO THE BAR: DRINKING ESTABLISHMENTS DURING THE COLONIAL AND POSTCOLONIAL PERIODS

There were a number of types of drinking establishments in the Americas during the colonial and postcolonial periods, including juke joints, honky-tonks, taverns, pulquerias, and cantinas. The distinctions between these establishments were based on a combination of alcohol type, social class, ethnicity, and race.

The juke joint in Central America was an "entertainment maroon" that allowed Black workers to temporarily escape the harsh conditions of life as railroad and banana plantation workers. The position of Black men in early twentieth century Guatemalan society was ambiguous. Many Blacks in Guatemala were U.S. citizens and had minimally more rights than they did in the U.S. South under Jim Crow laws. The U.S. State Department had a vested interest in protecting U.S. citizens and capital, and thus Black laborers sought aid from U.S. diplomats when labor abuse occurred, though not always successfully.[39] However, the United Fruit Company imposed a Jim Crow–like hierarchy on its lands that did not treat Blacks as equal to whites.[40] The juke joint was a place where Black workers could hear American jazz and avoid the discrimination that was otherwise pervasive.[41] The honky-tonk was usually a whites-only juke joint that played country music.[42] Outside of white areas, honky-tonks were Black spaces or, minimally, non–Jim Crow spaces.[43] Rum shops, sometimes attached to homes, acted as stripped-down versions of juke joints and honky-tonks, providing drinks but fewer amenities and a lower startup cost for owners.[44]

Taverns were the first European-influenced drinking establishments that primarily served wines and brandies imported into the area.[45] Like other drinking establishments, they were known for attracting "loose women."[46] Taverns sometimes refused to sell their imported alcohol to Indigenous men, imposing a social stratification within the lower classes.[47] The Guatemalan *vinatería* sought an upper-crust audience of both men and women.[48] Although there was racial mixing, colonial city laws explicitly forbade the sale of aguardiente and wines of Spain and Peru to Indigenous people.[49]

Starting in the mid-nineteenth century in central México, elite white women owned pulquerias that were supplied by pulque produced on their own large landholdings. They were often the relatives of male pulque entrepreneurs and had to hire male administrators to be the face of their businesses. The social spaces of pulquerias were restricted to men, and poor Indigenous women sold prepared foods on the streets outside as a way to earn a living.[50] They made agreements with the female tavern owners to sell cheap and fast food, such as tacos, mole, and enchiladas, outside of the establishments. The owners preferred spicy food on the menu, as it increased the amount of pulque that patrons drank. This was also appealing because much of the working poor lacked cooking facilities or simply didn't have time to prepare meals, and it was a socially acceptable role for women who needed to make an income outside the household.[51] Inside the tavern, they sold pulque. While pure pulque (*pulque puro* or *pulque blanco*) remained associated with "Indian-ness," pulque mixed with other substances became an indicator of hybridity.[52] Lower-class Spaniards drank it with Indigenous people and Blacks, in public and in private.[53]

## THE CANTINA IN YUCATÁN

The Yucatecan cantina (figures 26 and 27) borrows elements from these types of drinking venues, especially the tavern's association with loose women and the juke joints' music and role as a place to enjoy a temporary escape from life.[54] By the 1850s, cantinas developed in urban spaces as places where lower-class men could go to escape the rigors of their lives. Unfortunately, there are virtually no sources of information for understanding social interactions within these nineteenth-century cantinas. Thus we must turn to the few contemporary sources that exist as admittedly limited models for understanding these establishments as social spaces.

**FIGURE 26.** Historic La Cantina Sabrosa still doing business in Mérida today. (Photograph by John R. Gust.)

**FIGURE 27.** Historic Cantina El Cardenal open nightly in Mérida. (Photograph by John R. Gust.)

Among Mexican men, machismo (showing independence and dominance over women, sexual virility, as well as demonstrating hypermasculinity) and manhood are associated with drinking and friendship, and Mexican cantinas serve as a gendered social space.[55] For men, it was a place to dance, arrange sexual encounters, and gossip with their male friends. The cantina served as a space for the rite of passage of engaging in male misbehavior and as a social outlet. "One of the primary reasons that a person enters the cantina is to interact with others in ways that would be socially unacceptable within other social settings," in part because of the high rate of alcohol consumption.[56] The setting usually includes jukeboxes or live musicians who play loud music, with men sitting at barstools or small tables.[57] However, as Stross states, "It is also common knowledge that 'decent women do not enter the cantina,'" automatically denigrating women who are present within cantinas as disreputable.[58]

## WOMEN IN CANTINAS

The image of the cantina woman is thus counter to the traditional role of women under *marianismo*—the belief that women should be valued in their role as mothers, and for their focus on the family and the home. They are expected to encourage family cohesion through self-sacrifice; be loyal, virtuous, and chaste; show moral strength; and demonstrate obedience to the male hierarchy.[59] As Stross states, "The cantina woman . . . usually has one or more illegitimate children to support, smokes, drinks, curses, sells her body, stares invitingly at a man without feeling shame, fights in jest or in earnest, and often playfully grabs at the private parts of her female co-workers."[60] He also says that cantina women may be teased or asked intimate questions, spoken to in a way that is normally reserved for men, or totally ignored. And yet she is also desired for being everything that a proper woman is not.[61]

A 1990s study of Mexican cantinas in Southern California examined the role of women in these establishments. These male spaces usually included female employees, including *cantineras*, or barmaids; *ficheras*, or dancers; and *taloneras*, or sex workers.[62] The category of cantineras seems to be a more recent phenomenon, as Stross identifies waiters in Mexican cantinas in the 1960s exclusively as males between the ages of twenty-five to forty-five.[63] In southern California, waiters may be women or men, but cantineras are specifically women who wait on tables for tips, push the sale of drinks, and while they are often fondled by male patrons, they generally do not have sex with them. However, the role of the cantineros/cantineras does seem to have the common characteristics of maintaining social order. Regardless of gender, they are expected to be pleasing to their customers by listening to them and providing them with food and drinks. They are also expected to be ready to deal with problems, such as customers engaging in violent behavior or calming customers down when policemen enter the space.[64] Cantineras further serve as a symbol of the client's wife or girlfriend, upon which he can hurl insults and hostilities without punishment.[65]

The role of the fichera is to get men to dance with them. Men generally initiate the encounter with a gesture or by going up to ask an unoccupied woman to dance, although she does have the right to refuse him.[66] Once the dance is complete, the man can either return to his table alone or ask the fichera to join him at the table for a drink. For every drink sold, the bartender or waiter will give her a token (ficha), which she can convert to cash at a later time.[67] The fichera will also allow the men to fondle her, although she will only stay at the table as long as she has a drink, and she will move on to another patron once her current prospect runs out of money.[68] This is purely business for them, and the women generally protect their individuality by exhibiting a kind of social distance from their clients.[69] Conversely, men are more likely to confide personal subjects and feelings to women in cantinas (and to waiters and bartenders as well), which is socially acceptable because of their excessive drinking.[70] Men can also learn to dance without embarrassment, as they are not concerned about what the cantina women think of them.[71] While the fichera may also negotiate money for sex with her client, he must pay an exit fee to the waiter to do so.[72] In the United States, although the fichera may negotiate sex with a client around closing time, it is the talonera that primarily serves as a sex worker in cantinas, although this would not be applicable in the nineteenth century onward.[73]

The cantinas offered the safest space for male patrons and sex workers to arrange sexual encounters (to be held elsewhere), as they are less likely to encounter police there than on the streets where sex workers frequented. Interviews with cantina sex workers in California revealed that they generally felt that their clients were men looking for companionship and someone who could get drunk with them. They stated that their needs for sex were not being met by their wives and that they asked prostitutes to engage in oral sex because their wives would not do it.[74] The price was negotiated based on the age and attractiveness of the woman, although a man might have been considered more macho if he could negotiate a price down due to his charm or manliness.[75]

## WOMEN OUTSIDE OF CANTINAS

For the wives and children of male cantina patrons, the cantina represented a dangerous space that resulted in physical abuse, rape, and violence. One source for understanding these issues is to review the testimonials of women who have been subject to alcohol-fueled abuse. Award-winning playwright Petrona de la Cruz Cruz, a Maya woman from Chiapas, wrote a biographical play called "*Una Mujer Desesperada*" ("A Desperate Woman"), as a way to discuss the struggles of Indigenous women and children in daily life. She raised issues related to the violence, rape, and poverty that often stemmed from men's alcohol abuse.[76] The play opened with a hungry mother holding a sick daughter and talking about an absent father. "Their father has never cared about them. He doesn't even remember to bring them food. He lives in the cantina with his friends."[77] The implication is that because of alcohol abuse, husbands and fathers don't work, and they spend the money that they do have in the cantinas rather than providing for their families.[78] When they return home drunk, it is their families who suffer. "Don't you understand, man? How can I make a fire if we don't have kindling or food [*sic*]. You are so drunk that you don't see anything. You haven't worked for a long time, even to feed your daughters. Look how sick they are, and you just keep getting drunk and throwing away money that we don't have."[79]

This stoic acceptance of men's misbehavior and the resulting women's suffering stems from the colonial period, during which women were expected to emulate the Virgin Mary (marianismo). The Spanish limited women's rights and social roles through laws and social codes, emphasizing their realm as spiritual and secondary within the context of the home, church, and family. This was juxtaposed with the image of *La Malinche*, the vilified mistress of Hernan Cortes, who demonstrated what happened when a woman sought a public and liberated role.[80]

In the context of the nineteenth-century hacienda and machismo, we also know that many of those male abuses went unpunished.[81] "Judges— usually planters or their clients—appreciated the notion that if every infraction, drunk or sober, received a 'just' sentence, the jails would overflow, and few laborers would be left to work in the henequen fields."[82] In highland Guatemala in the nineteenth century, dictatorial regimes overlooked or even pardoned drunken men who beat their wives.[83]

## POSTREVOLUTIONARY ALCOHOL POLICY, WOMEN, AND THE CANTINA

Despite their willingness to ignore alcohol-fueled violence, the postrevolutionary government in Yucatán understood other negative effects of alcohol on the lower class.[84] In 1915, the military governor of Yucatán, General Salvador Alvarado, signed a group of protective laws, collectively known as *La Ley Seca* (Dry Law) that limited the production and sale of alcohol. This first law made the sale of liquor to minors and women illegal. The second law stopped women from working in cantinas, limited the sale of alcohol in restaurants and grills, and mandated that cantinas located too close to schools must move. The third law outlawed the sale of alcohol in cantinas during national holidays, Sundays, after ten at night, and during siesta break. When these laws did not significantly change drinking patterns, General Alvarado outlawed the sale and production of aguardiente entirely. Although drinks with low alcohol content, like beer, remained legal, this "ended the golden age of the domestic rum industry in Yucatán."[85]

When President Venustiano Carranza (1917–20) ordered Alvarado out of Yucatán, the Ley Seca remained on the books. However, the law was inconsistently applied, and enforcement became a tool wielded against political and business enemies.[86] Alcohol remained a tool to encourage members of opposition parties to defect to the causes of the Socialist Party and facilitated bootlegging, which corrupt party leaders turned into a source of income.[87] Even after enforcement of the Dry Law diminished, women often led temperance plans, resulting in the prohibition of liquor in a number of villages and towns.[88] Other reforms, some alcohol-related, directly affected women. In addition to women being barred from employment in cantinas, sex work was more heavily scrutinized both legally and by medical professionals.[89] Some of these reforms were new, and others built upon existing Porfirian trends toward pathologizing the bodies of Indigenous women and their traditional health practices.[90] Reforms recognized drunkenness as legal grounds for divorce.[91] They also warned men of the dangers of sexually transmitted infections for both themselves and their families and that having sex while drunk could result in the conception of a child with cognitive defects.[92] Thus revolutionary reforms had mixed results for women. Married women and those living with partners were granted extended rights, but sex workers' financial well-being was further undermined in a society that offered little opportunity for unattached women.

During the late nineteenth century, Yucatecan hacienda owners controlled laborers' access to rum by jacking up prices and increasing their debt, rather than legislating on the basis of morality or health. This debt and resulting lack of social freedoms increased the stress of Indigenous families, with women and children paying the greatest price through violence and economic hardship. While rum did provide some economic benefits to those women who could manage cantinas, engage in sex work with cantina patrons, or sell food outside of the establishments, ultimately their social and economic status was at the whim of the government and the male patrons on whom they depended. During the early twentieth century, domestic laws meant to protect the lower class and women and children were enacted. However, this drove the alcohol industry underground, further eroding the stability of women already living on the periphery of society.

In the late twentieth and early twenty-first century, rum and other alcohol continued to have the same social and economic effects on the Yucatán Peninsula. Differences in the local economies of the areas where rum was produced in the nineteenth century (the east coast of the peninsula, where Cancun is now located, and the Mérida area, where the henequen industry flourished) are reflected in the variety of tourism development strategies that operate in these regions today.

## RUM AS METAPHOR: CANCÚN VERSUS MÉRIDA

The recent history of Quintana Roo in eastern Yucatán is one of boom and bust. Tourism is not the first industry focused on products for export to other regions or countries that operate there. In reliable succession, the hardwood, cattle, sugar and rum, and chicle industries have exploited the plants and Maya of Quintana Roo for centuries. These businesses took advantage of the populations, economies, and infrastructures while business was booming, and then abandoned them when business failed.[93] Tourism is the latest of these industries and is linked to both the area's past as a rum producer and the lack of a preexisting sense of place. The effects of tourism on Quintana Roo are most evident in the greater Cancún area.

We argue that rum is a metaphor for Cancún, and the city represents temporary escape in much the same way as a bottle of aguardiente allowed a debt peon a respite from life. Specifically, this comparison applies to the cheap well rum that comes as part of spring break packages and with trips to the all-inclusive resorts. The free-flowing fruity drinks that hide the taste of inferior rum are enjoyable and do not stress the palate of the drinker. Locals often refer to Cancún as "Gringolandia," alluding to its Disneyland-like qualities that mesh Mexican, U.S., and Maya culture in an artificial way.[94] Today, North American tourists can stay in their choice of approximately 150 hotels, eat at any of the roughly 400 restaurants, and feel like they have never left home. In the Hotel Zone, tourists generally do not need to exchange dollars for pesos, the majority of employees speak at least some English, and the city sports several Walmart stores, a Sam's Club, and Costco. Visitors can find nearly every kind of fast-food and chain restaurant imaginable, from the ubiquitous McDonald's to TGI Fridays, (the non-ironically-intended) Rainforest Café, and Hard Rock Café (figure 28). Most tourism in Cancún is just like the mass-produced rum that is poured there: consistent but rarely exciting.

**FIGURE 28.** American restaurants in Cancún Hotel Zone. (Photograph by John R. Gust.)

In large population centers of western Yucatán, the tourism sector is dominated by small locally owned hotels and restaurants. Mérida, the capital, has chain hotels, but they are primarily located outside or at the fringe of tourist areas, and independent hotels are plentiful and usually more affordable than corporate options. This local ownership contrasts with Cancún, where ownership by national or transnational corporations concentrates profits within a small group of people and establishments that focus on providing a Western-style experience. Such establishments in Cancún employ Yucatán natives, mostly in the lower-paying and seasonal positions, while better-paying and permanent positions are staffed by educated (and non-Indigenous-looking) people from elsewhere in México or abroad.[95] While Cancún might be seen as the equivalent of mass-produced rum that the majority of tourists might enjoy, Mérida represents the craft distillery, content to produce a limited supply of high-quality rum that is marketed to connoisseurs. In fact, one such distillery exists in Mérida: Casa D'Aristi makes small-batch rum-based spirits by incorporating the ingredients of Yucatán, such as honey, anise, coconut milk, and soursop.[96] Such rums and liqueurs may be inconsistent batch to batch but are more interesting because they are unique. An "alternative" vacation to Yucatán will always be just as unpredictable. The gross division between these two populations of visitors has been described as "mass" versus "alternative" tourism.[97] Mass tourists are visitors who want "Western amenities, good infrastructure," and a reliably enjoyable trip.[98] As a "stay in a hotel room is 'an experience good'" (meaning that unlike most goods, it cannot be closely inspected before being consumed), there is a benefit to staying in a chain hotel that should be expected to meet certain standards, regardless of location.[99]

## THE DEVELOPMENT OF CANCÚN

Before the 1970s, few outsiders other than adventurers, archaeologists, and divers came to Quintana Roo.[100] So how did the region go from a secret hideaway to the "Maya Riviera" of today? In 1969, the Mexican government asked the Bank of México and FONATUR (*Fondo Nacional de Fomento al Turismo*), the national agency in charge of tourism, to conduct a study on the tourism of México. They concluded that the country had far too few developed tourism areas and wanted to attract more visitors— particularly those from the United States.[101] Using a computer program and reconnaissance teams, they examined more than six thousand miles of Mexican coastline in search of areas with great year-round weather; few hurricane scares; available drinking water; a low incidence of sharks, bugs, or snakes; and picturesque beaches lapped by deep blue waters. All things being equal, they also wanted to locate the new resorts in areas where there was an ample labor supply and a local population that was poor and in need of low-skilled employment.[102] The government also hoped to avoid another Acapulco, which was plagued with polluted waters and the location of shanty towns next to upscale resorts, by regulating the outpouring of toxins into the water supply and minimizing unzoned growth.[103]

The research team chose the island of Cancún (with plans to develop Ixtapa on the Pacific Coast, Los Cabos and Loreto in Baja California, and Bahías de Huatulco in Oaxaca soon after), and the government bought up the entire 14 km L-shaped island. Cancún was an ideal candidate with almost no previous development, coral sand beaches (figure 29), an ample freshwater source, ancient Maya ruins (sites include Tulum, which is approximately 130 km away; Chichén Itzá, which is 200 km away; and Cobá, which is 172 km away), an annual average temperature of 85 degrees and sunshine an average of 243 days a year, and no history of direct hits from hurricanes.[104] Additionally, the proximity of Cancún to major cities in the United States made it one of the most convenient tourism centers in the Caribbean.[105] The team funneled private and government funding totaling a hundred million dollars into constructing the resort area concentrated on the small island in various development stages, and the Hotel Zone was built to be set apart from the city proper.[106] By 1973, the team planned to build a permanent two-hundred-foot-long bridge

**FIGURE 29.** Beach in Cancún Hotel Zone, Quintana Roo. (Copyright Macduff Everton 2019, image 01136.)

to connect the island to the rest of the coast; install a sewage-treatment plant; pipe in fresh water from the mainland; and build a harbor and marina, a convention center, two eighteen-hole golf courses, several small hotels, a shopping area (with Maya architectural themes), and an international airport twenty-four kilometers away.[107]

Torres finds Fordist analysis of mass production to be a useful, if imperfect, tool for understanding the touristic development of Yucatán.[108] This enclavic style of mass tourism isolates the visitor from the normal issues of daily life, both their own and those of the people of the host country.[109] Cancún developers hoped that by 1975 they would have created ten thousand permanent jobs for the local, primarily Maya, population to sustain this new tourist hot spot.[110] However, they created an intentional division between the resorts and the supporting infrastructure by constructing supermarkets, small businesses, and 670 buildings to house workers away from the tourist enclave.[111]

In 1975, eight hundred new working families were moving to Cancún every month, only 12 percent of whom had been born in the state of Quintana Roo.[112] While local government workers were housed in a planned area maintained by FONATUR just adjacent to the resort area, service workers were intentionally segregated and lived on the margins of downtown in concrete apartment buildings that could be constructed vertically and horizontally as needed.[113] Many of these service-sector areas, including a squatter settlement of tar-paper shacks that later developed in the Cancún neighborhood of Colonia Puerto Juárez, have been slow to receive services such as electricity, water, sewage, and paved roads.[114] By 1980, the sleepy fishing village of Cancún that once had 800 residents had become a city of 50,000 people, and this was in a state that claimed a total population of 50,169 in 1960.[115] Although a 1982 development program known as "Nuevos Horizontes" attempted to improve basic services for the earliest squatter settlements, the majority of these low-wage laborers continued to live in squalor and do so to this day.[116]

Hiernaux-Nicolás describes this development of Cancún as quasi-utopian, especially in the case of the all-inclusive resort.[117] The word *utopia*, first coined by Sir Thomas More in 1516, is based on the Greek *ou–topos*, meaning "nowhere or no place."[118] Thus the isolation of the resorts and the standardized Western-style infrastructure meets tourists' desires, but at the cost of being generic. All-inclusive resorts further distance tourists from the locality and its inhabitants, as travel packages draw tourists seeking predictability both in terms of service and cost.[119]

**FIGURE 30.** Ancient site of Tulum, overlooking the Caribbean Sea. (Photograph by Jennifer P. Mathews.)

Arguably these are also "get away from it all" tourists, who want to push as many decisions off on others as possible. Although usually with a nod to luxury, most all-inclusive resorts lack cultural distinction and can be constructed almost anywhere with a similar climate. These tourism areas also isolate themselves from the surrounding cultural zone and everyday life. In fact, the Hotel Zone is even exempt from the laws that restrict public alcohol sales during elections for everywhere else in México (aside from a few other tourist zones).[120]

Continuing the Fordist analysis, Torres describes how tourists eventually demanded greater flexibility in their vacation experience.[121] This demand has usually been met by allowing the tourist to choose from a limited menu of options of preplanned excursions either run by the hotel itself or through its subcontractors. When surveyed, mass tourists ranked shopping trips higher than exploring on their own or visiting nature reserves, although they did show a strong interest in visiting archaeological sites (figure 30).[122] As Torres notes, however, the sites that they choose to visit have gift shops, restaurants, and other modern amenities, and can be traveled to and from in air-conditioned buses and vans.[123] Thus Torres describes these demands as a kind of neo-Fordism that offers flexibility within constraints.[124] In practice, the hotel operator has a financial stake in responding to demands for flexibility in ways in that can be controlled. Not only does the hotel or resort staff want to capture a portion of the proceeds from the trip, but they also are aware that any accidents or incidents involving tourists can harm the reputation of their hotel or resort. One way to limit the time spent outside of the hotel's purview is to bundle some activities within the price of a travel package.[125] Tourists who choose activities not included in the package price do so at additional cost.

## TOURISM DEVELOPMENT IN MÉRIDA

The capital city of Mérida in the state of Yucatán stands in contrast to Cancún and the Maya Riviera. The largest city on the Yucatán Peninsula, it is located in the northwest corner of the peninsula. Unlike the zoning in Cancún's Hotel Zone, which took into consideration the "cumulative visual effect" of all the hotels, resorts near Mérida are usually on renovated hacienda land and play on the uniqueness of the place and history of the area.[126] Hotels and restaurants in the central (historic) district of Mérida are housed within renovated colonial-period structures, again making the history part of the experience. While many servers and other low-level staff are originally from small villages, the owners of hotels and restaurants are usually either long-term residents of the city or people who lived in the city for years and then opened a business. Visitors to tourist-related establishments within Mérida will find that many in the service industry speak English, although it is generally Spanish-only in the smaller restaurants and hotels that primarily cater to Mexican tourists. In contrast to the wide streets of Cancún's Hotel Zone, the streets of Mérida are narrow and lined with uneven sidewalks full of people sliding past each other as they go to work or go shopping. Unless the visitor purposefully stays at a spa outside the city, they will encounter people going about their normal day and will eat next to Mexican families in the restaurants at night.

Although there are a large number of luxury hotel rooms (known as *gran turismo*) in the Cancún area, there are also deluxe accommodations in the Mérida area.[127] However, Cancún's luxury offerings are more affordable because they are available on a mass scale, while Mérida's are more expensive because they are unique and tailored to appealing to those interested in staying within a historic context. The variety of accommodations available in Mérida mesh well with travelers of various incomes who are more interested in exploring on their own in a more impromptu fashion, versus those who would rather choose from tours with preplanned activities. The historic and memorable character of Mérida's restaurants, hotels, and spas not only allows the tourist to see history but also repeat history via the continuing cycle of inequality in the workforce. For example, hacienda resorts are staffed by Indigenous people but are owned by wealthy mestizos and managed by foreigners— often Europeans.[128] This hierarchy recapitulates the labor structure of the hacienda and hacienda period. The Maya still do the grunt work for the benefit of wealthy mestizos and their guests.

## CONCLUSIONS

In this chapter we have primarily investigated the continuing effects of a social system influenced by rum production on those who were not working directly within the industry. We have seen how powerful figures in Yucatán complained about drunkenness among their workers and the working class at large, but failed to take action to effect change. Often the hacienda owners themselves were the sellers of rum to their workers and, in many cases, the only sources through which workers could consistently access it. Had they been so inclined, hacienda owners could have "dried" up the supply of rum. However, the operating costs of haciendas seemingly necessitated both using entrapped labor and turning a profit in company stores—hence securing the place of rum as a staple in working-class society. Thus hacienda owners complained about drunkenness among workers but failed to take steps to curtail it. Instead, it appears that the problems associated with alcohol were part and parcel of the hacienda system and, as the hacienda owners and henequen brokers were also often political leaders, a direct result of state practice. The economic system of Yucatán, especially during the henequen boom, was predicated on a pliant workforce. The availability of alcohol also gave workers a "safe" outlet for venting their frustrations while not in their right mind. Inappropriate behavior while sober would have been punished severely, but the ravings of a drunk were usually dismissed. The families of workers suffered the most, enduring abuse and hunger due to the loss of wages that went to alcohol. Drunkenness also divided loyalties among workers, helping ensure against concerted resistance such as strikes or revolts.

Alcohol—in particular, the drink of the masses, aguardiente rum— acted as a social glue, a social repellent, and a social lubricant. The ruling class of Yucatán managed to profit from alcohol production while ignoring the most onerous of the problems created by the abuse of alcohol in the working class. The centrality of rum was not lost on the postrevolutionary leaders of Yucatán. The Dry Law was partially intended to help free workers from oppression and spur advancement, but in ways often antagonistic to Maya culture instead of in support of it. Women emerged as temperance leaders, and some towns and villages banned alcoholic beverages. The availability of so much as a beer with dinner is still spotty in many small villages of Yucatán today as a result. The Dry Law also undercut the only source of income for sex workers in the cantinas.

In the twentieth century, we see the rise of tourism that develops on two separate paths in the eastern and western sides of the peninsula. Cancún is a segregated city with the tourist zone built around a drinking culture. The heart of the Hotel Zone is based on bars, clubs, and all-inclusive resorts with "all-you-can-drink" packages intended to keep tourists on the island. The focus is on U.S. tourists who are interested in having modern conveniences that won't take them out of their comfort zones and won't expose them to daily life among the city's poor.

What Cancun obscures, Mérida sells. To go to Mérida is to interact with its history, or a version of it at least. You will hear much more Spanish spoken in the tourist areas. The park in the historic center is full of small vendors, but you still will find a few beggars. The restaurants and shops are mostly in converted historic homes and businesses that are well kept but still show their age. The furnishings are reminiscent of hacienda life and often include repurposed detritus from the hacienda itself. The visitor to Mérida is immersed in the remnants of a system that built Yucatán into one of México's richest regions on the backs of the poor and sustains the social hierarchy that has disadvantaged the Yucatec Maya for centuries.

# CONCLUSION
## AND IMPLICATIONS FOR THE FUTURE

THE IMPORTANCE OF SUGARCANE AND rum in the history of Yucatán fluctuates through time, as does the visibility of their impacts on Yucatán. This work is part of a growing body of research that attempts to track the importance of a commodity on a place in its history.[1] The difference between this text and most other similar works is that while rum and sugar are crucial to the economy of Yucatán, it was henequen that generated the wealth of the region. In this work we argue that rum (and sugar) are critical to understanding the history of Yucatán after European contact and that the relationship of the working class to these commodities has influenced the history of Yucatán in times of change and relative stability. The relationship between rum, Yucatecan elites in the planter class, and the working class is only part of the story, as rum is also a subject of official state policy created by the governmental leadership of Yucatán, who in some cases were also planters.

The first attempts to grow sugar in Yucatán occurred in the 1530s after the region was brought under the control of Spain but ended abruptly when the Montejo family was stripped of their encomienda for their extreme abuses of the native population.[2] For nearly 250 years, aguardiente rum and sugar were two of the most imported goods in Yucatán. There is little documentation about sugar production in Yucatán during this period, although there were complaints that sugarcane farming monopolized laborers, leaving too few for other uses. In response, the government banned aguardiente production on the peninsula, although it was still imported and produced illegally on a small scale.[3]

By 1740, the government justified the need to expropriate town and village lands to accommodate a growing population and as a way to control the Maya working population. As the Maya could no longer support themselves through farming on communal lands, many chose to attach themselves to haciendas through debt peonage. Although those working sugar in the Caribbean and Brazil worked within the confines of slavery, Yucatecan sugar laborers experienced a similar level of brutality. In 1843, the government made debt peonage, which hacienda owners practiced unofficially for decades, a legal mechanism to bind indebted workers.[4] The abusive conditions led to a Maya revolt in 1847, and Caste War rebels especially targeted sugar haciendas because of the visible profitability of sugar haciendas in comparison to other ventures.[5] Although the southeast portion of the peninsula stayed in the hands of Caste War rebels (headquartered in Chan Santa Cruz) until 1901, much of the rest of the peninsula was back under the control of the government of Yucatán by the 1850s.[6] Villagers and townspeople in some areas agreed to make peace with the government, including Kantunilkin, the largest town in the Yalahau region.[7]

Soils of the Yalahau region are moderately well-suited for growing sugarcane, and a number of ventures for growing sugarcane and distilling rum were opened in the 1870s in and around Kantunilkin.[8] The resulting rum ended up in company stores on henequen haciendas and in Mérida bars and cantinas.[9] These spaces provided opportunities for women to engage in sex work, low-status bar work, or street food vending, some of the only opportunities for unattached women to make a living or supplement their family income.[10]

After the Mexican Revolution ended, the political and military leaders of Yucatán understood the role of aguardiente in entrapping workers into peonage. They passed reforms to regulate cantinas, making it illegal for women to work in them, and limit aguardiente consumption, eventually prohibiting its production altogether. These laws were selectively applied against political rivals, undermined unattached women's financial security, and ultimately led to the banning of rum production, driving it underground.[11] The government and elites of Yucatán have regulated and controlled rum as a matter of public policy and economic practice since the peninsula fell under Spanish and then Yucatecan control. The elite viewed the means of production as an industry that benefited the rich, and rum ultimately became a tool of social control.

Today, much of the Yucatán Peninsula's economy is focused on tourism, importing visitors temporarily, rather than on the export of commodities.[12] In an interesting twist, tourism in and around Mérida has romanticized haciendas and colonial buildings by highlighting their historical past and converting them into upscale hotels and spas.[13] High-end rum is used to attract visitors, the old processing equipment is used as decoration, and tourists can even ride the old Decauville trams around the hacienda grounds. In contrast, the land on which Cancún now sits was chosen in part because there was no existing infrastructure and the Mexican government could develop the area into whatever they wanted it to be.[14] By inviting large, well-capitalized hotel chains to do business there, planners made Cancún an affordable destination that could attract large numbers of tourists—all who could be expected to experience a predictable vacation.[15] The hotels and resorts in Cancún and the Maya Riviera emphasize their newness and modern conveniences, as there were no recent historic buildings to transform.[16] They highlight bars and clubs that sell cheap rum drinks and travel in which visitors are not burdened with having to make decisions but rather follow a preplanned itinerary.[17]

Sugar and rum have clearly been secondary commodities as compared with the "green gold" of the henequen industry that brought tremendous wealth to the western half of the Yucatán Peninsula.[18] And yet rum and sugar have held a significant presence in the social structure of Yucatán since the arrival of the Spanish and, in less obvious ways, have left an indelible mark on the region. Whether consumed as harsh well rum masked by a fruity concoction in a resort in Cancún or in the form of a glass of high-quality, small-batch rum sipped in a remodeled former hacienda, rum and its effects are ever present on the built environment and landscape of Yucatán.

# APPENDIX

## REFERENCE TABLES

**TABLE 1.** Number of weeks worked by San Eusebio salarios and jornaleros, in four-week increments

| WEEKS WORKED | NUMBER OF WORKERS | PERCENTAGE OF WORKERS |
|---|---|---|
| 1 to 4 | 153 | 64.83 |
| 5 to 8 | 18 | 7.63 |
| 9 to 12 | 18 | 7.63 |
| 13 to 16 | 8 | 3.39 |
| 17 to 20 | 7 | 2.97 |
| 21 to 24 | 13 | 5.51 |
| 25 to 28 | 13 | 5.51 |
| 29 to 32 | 6 | 2.54 |
| Total | 236 | 100.00 |

**TABLE 2.** Function-based artifact typology for Xuxub artifact assemblage

| | | XUXUB ARTIFACTS | |
|---|---|---|---|
| CATEGORY | WEIGHT (G) | CATEGORY TOTAL WEIGHT (G) | PERCENTAGE OF TOTAL ASSEMBLAGE |
| **Recreation** | | 7,952 | 28.62 |
| Alcohol | 7,952 | | |
| **Building material** | | 5,754 | 20.71 |
| Brick | 782 | | |
| Flooring | 4,360 | | |
| Roofing | 612 | | |
| **Personal** | | 5,068 | 18.24 |
| Adornment | 4,634 | | |
| Consumption | 59 | | |
| Medicine/ cosmetics | 375 | | |
| **Subsistence** | | 4,589 | 16.52 |
| Consumption | 1,096 | | |
| Preparation | 3,394 | | |
| Storage | 99 | | |
| **Hardware** | | 1,124 | 4.05 |
| Fasteners/wire | 1,098 | | |
| Tools | 26 | | |
| **Local ceramics** | | 894 | 3.22 |
| Local ancient | 54 | | |
| Local recent | 840 | | |
| **Faunal remains** | | 30 | 0.11 |
| Fauna | 30 | | |
| **Other/ indeterminate** | | 2,372 | 8.54 |
| Total | | 27,783 | 100.00 |

**TABLE 3.** Function-based artifact typology for San Eusebio artifact assemblage

| | SAN EUSEBIO ARTIFACTS | | |
|---|---|---|---|
| CATEGORY | WEIGHT (G) | CATEGORY TOTAL WEIGHT (G) | PERCENTAGE OF TOTAL ASSEMBLAGE |
| **Personal** | | 8,998 | 32.80 |
| Adornment | 8,349 | | |
| Clothing | 25 | | |
| Indeterminate | 60 | | |
| Medicine/ cosmetics | 579 | | |
| **Recreation** | | 6,019 | 21.94 |
| Alcohol | 6,012 | | |
| Tobacco | 7 | | |
| **Building material** | | 4,271 | 15.57 |
| Brick | | | |
| Flooring | 106 | | |
| Roofing | 28 | | |
| Stucco | 78 | | |
| **Hardware** | | 2,072 | 7.55 |
| Fasteners | 217 | | |
| Indeterminate | 297 | | |
| Machine part | 261 | | |
| Railroad | 72 | | |
| Supplies | 759 | | |
| Tools | 466 | | |
| **Subsistence** | | 1,734 | 6.32 |
| Consumption | 449 | | |

*continued*

**TABLE 3.** *continued*

| CATEGORY | WEIGHT (G) | CATEGORY TOTAL WEIGHT (G) | PERCENTAGE OF TOTAL ASSEMBLAGE |
|---|---|---|---|
| Indeterminate | 9 | | |
| Preparation | 482 | | |
| Procurement | 18 | | |
| Storage | 776 | | |
| **Faunal remains** | | 1,372 | 5.00 |
| **Local ceramics** | | 591 | 2.15 |
| Ancient | 90 | | |
| Recent | 501 | | |
| **Other/ indeterminate** | | 2,377 | 8.66 |
| Total | | 27,434 | 100.00 |

# NOTES

## INTRODUCTION

1. Throughout this work, *sugar* and *rum* refer to manufactured goods made from cultivated sugarcane.
2. Alston, Mattiace, and Nonnenmacher 2009, 11.
3. Meyers and Carlson 2002, 229.
4. Taylor 1979, 27.
5. Scott 1985.
6. Here, *haciendas* refers to factory farms.
7. Standing 2014.
8. Mathews and Gust 2017; Gust 2016; Sullivan 2004, 16, 23.
9. As Sullivan (2004, 29) notes, the manager of the Xuxub hacienda in Quintana Roo feared violence from a local mayor whom he believed was working on behalf of the Urcelay family—owners of the adjacent sugar hacienda.
10. Foss 2012, 83; Rogoziński 1999, 109.
11. This was at least partially true, as the colonies and their shipping routes were protected by navy ships.
12. In Jamaica planters depended on the British military to protect them from their slaves (Petley 2005, 102).
13. Williams 2005, 125–29, 160.
14. A *plantocracy* is a population of planters regarded as the dominant class.
15. Rivero 1994, 57.
16. Brannon and Baklanoff 1987, xi; Lucien 2014, 6.

17. Ian Williams (2005, 11) came to this same conclusion independently.
18. North of the current state of Quintana Roo.
19. This is currently the near-unanimous consensus opinion, but Zizumbo-Villarreal et al. (2009) argue a mechanism for distillation in western Mesoamerica before European contact. If true, such a mechanism could have been used to distill liquor.
20. Schwartzkopf 2017, 60, 66.
21. Celaya and Owen 1993, 441, in Pi-Sunyer and Thomas 1999, 16.
22. Torres and Momsen 2004, especially 303–7.
23. Hiernaux-Nicolás 1999, 131.
24. Torres and Momsen 2004, especially 303–7.
25. Fallaw 2002, 43.

## CHAPTER I

1. Ratekin 1954, 1.
2. Koeppel 2008.
3. Barnes 1964, 1–2.
4. Nicol 2003, 263. Deerr (1949, 17) reports that the earliest entry on sugarcane in Chinese written records dates to 286 CE. See also Barty-King and Massel 1983, 3; Barnes 1964, 2.
5. Mintz 1985, 20.
6. Mintz 1985, 20–23.
7. Mintz 1985, 78.
8. Kessler 2015, 136. Takeguchi et al. (1999) provide an earlier date of approximately 600 CE.
9. Kessler 2015, 136, 138.
10. Barty-King and Massel 1983, 3.
11. Ambler 2003, 76.
12. Mintz 1985, 32–33, 42–43; Ambler 2003, 73.
13. Foss 2012, 40. The same ships did not travel to all three points of the triangle, as slave ships were not ideal for other cargo, but that is the way the money flowed. A second triangle operated "[f]rom New England went rum to Africa, whence slaves to the West Indies, whence molasses back to New England (with which to make rum)," incorporating the New England rum trade into the world system (Mintz 1985, 43). See also Gjelten 2008, 17.
14. Nicol 2003, 263; Broom 2003, 10.
15. Williams 2005, 20.
16. Williams 2005, 21.

17. For the purposes of this chapter, we are defining *rum* as a distilled liquor made from sugarcane. This term thus encompasses such products as cachaça, aguardiente, kill devil, and so forth that meet this definition. Attempts at producing "rum" from sugar beets have resulted in poor taste and have generally been considered failures (Evans 1919, 237; Aykroyd 1967, 87; Foss 2012, 13; see also Evans 1919, 242). This spirit is not discussed further.

18. A fermented Indian sugar drink, *gaudi*, is mentioned in Sanskrit writings (Aykroyd 1967, 88).

19. Barty-King and Massel 1983.

20. Mintz 1985, xix, 32; Hagelberg 1985, 1.

21. Ratekin (1954, 1) reports that sugar was introduced to the island in 1493. Other scholars do not make this definitive claim, instead noting the production of sugar circa 1515–16 and presence of sugar cuttings on Columbus's second voyage in 1493, without citing 1493 as the year sugar was introduced to the island (Lockhart 1983, 75; Mintz 1985, 32; see also Smout 1961, 240).

22. Rogoziński 1999, 115–16.

23. Rogoziński 1999, 118.

24. Rogoziński 1999, 118.

25. Smout 1961, 240.

26. Barnes 1964, 87; Pang 1979, 670.

27. Pang 1979, 669–670; Roger 2010, 30.

28. Pang 1979, 670–671.

29. Lockhart and Schwartz 1983, 206.

30. Lockhart and Schwartz 1983, 202, 215.

31. Lockhart and Schwartz 1983, 206.

32. Lockhart and Schwartz 1983, 216.

33. Barty-King and Massel 1983, 117.

34. There is also near or complete overlap with cachaça and spirits marketed as sugarcane brandy. Sugarcane brandy, *ypioca*, is also marketed as cachaça. Williams 2005, 260.

35. Foss 2012, 27.

36. Allen Wells (1985, 22) and Howard Cline (1947, 51) cite 1605 as the early introduction date for sugar in Yucatán. And aside from its location in Champotón in Campeche, no more specific information about Montejo's sugar operation has been found. See also Patch 1993, 34.

37. Patch 2003, 34. Grants from the Spanish Crown allowing landowners to demand forced labor from Indigenous people in the Americas were later expanded to include tribute in goods (Lockhart 1969, 414; Zavala 1935). See also Abollado 2000, 17.

38. Patch 1993, 17, 34.

39. Patch (2003, 17) does not indicate where or when illicit cane alcohol production started.
40. Patch 1993, 142.
41. Williams 2005, 30; Smith and Watson 2009, 66.
42. The Spanish Main consists of Spain's coastal mainland territories surrounding the Gulf of México and Caribbean Sea. See Sheridan 1974, 125.
43. Williams 2005, 30.
44. These farms were still not considerably large, as more than two-thirds of the land was still in pieces smaller than two hundred acres (Sheridan 1974, 137).
45. Sheridan 1974, 132.
46. Williams 2005, 50.
47. Sheridan 1974, 132–33; Williams 2005, 49.
48. Sheridan 1974, 132–33.
49. Within the popular history of rum, Barbados has been cited as the place where the liquor was first made, and rum first appears in records from Barbados. Thus Barbados seems the most likely candidate for the birthplace of rum, but the evidence is not definitive.
50. Williams 2005, 29.
51. Barnes 1964, 99.
52. Satchell 2004, 37.
53. Satchell 2004, 37.
54. Satchell 2004, 37.
55. Foss 2012, 41.
56. Solomon 2009.
57. Satchell 2004, 38.
58. Barnes 1964, 99.
59. Satchell 2004, 37.
60. Rogoziński 1999, 118.
61. Oxford African American Studies Center 2010.
62. Rogoziński 1999, 121, 122.
63. Rogoziński 1999, 122.
64. Rogoziński 1999, 122.
65. Williams 2005, 265.
66. Foss 2012, 40, 51–52.
67. Foss 2012, 34.
68. Scarpaci 1975, 165.
69. Heitmann 1987, 9; Foss 2012, 49–50; Sitterson 1953, 94.
70. Sitterson 1953, 11.
71. Deerr 1949, 252; Foss 2012, 73.
72. Foss 2012, 73–74.

73. Smout 1961, 240.
74. Smout 1961, 240.
75. Gjelten 2008, 16; Rogoziński 1999, 122.
76. Gjelten 2008, 9, 16.
77. Martinez 1999, 57.
78. Bolland 1981, 594.
79. Hall 1971, 39.
80. Mintz 1995, 78.
81. Martinez 1999, 61.
82. Martinez 1999, 58–59.
83. Martinez 1999, 59.
84. Martinez 1999, 58.
85. Sitterson 1953, 205.
86. Sitterson 1953, 209.
87. Sitterson 1953, 233, 235.
88. Sitterson 1953, 234.
89. Sitterson 1953, 223.
90. Rodrigue 2001, 121, 125, 129.
91. Pang 1979, 671.
92. Pang 1979, 672–73; see also Rogers 2010, 40; Galloway 1989, 72; Schwartz 1978, 47–50; Miller 1989, 395; Lockhart and Schwartz 1983, 206, 216.
93. Pang 1979, 674.
94. Pang 1979, 676.
95. Pang 1979, 674–76.
96. Pang 1979, 681.
97. Pang 1979, 683.
98. Denslow 1975, 260.
99. Ninety-one percent of mills in Cuba were steam driven, compared to 4 percent in northeastern Brazil in 1858. Sixteen percent of Cuban mills used vacuum pans that made the boiling process more efficient, while northeastern Brazil had none (Denslow 1975, 260, 262).
100. Denslow 1975, 262–63.
101. Rogers 2010, 15, 74–78.
102. Barty-King and Massel 1983, 81.
103. Barty-King and Massel 1983, 82.
104. Rogoziński 1999, 119; Satchell 2004, 40.
105. Barty-King and Massel 1983, 91.
106. Sugar was grown, mostly on a small scale, in India for centuries. Distillation was refined, if not invented, in India. After slavery was abolished in the Caribbean, Indian laborers were contracted to work in places including Trinidad and Guyana. As with slave descendants elsewhere in the Carib-

bean, Indians have contributed to the population and cultural makeup of everywhere they were taken. See also Foss 2012, 45.
107. Satchell 2004, 39.
108. Tyson 1995, 136. Bolland discusses a similar contract system for Black lumber workers in Belize, where Kray has also found evidence of an unofficial system of debt peonage (Berleant-Schiller 1995, 57).
109. Berleant-Schiller 1995, 57.
110. Berleant-Schiller 1995, 61–62.
111. Berleant-Schiller 1995, 64.
112. Rodrigue 2001, 115–16, 133–34.
113. Rodrigue 2001, 116–17.
114. Rodrigue 2002, 124.
115. Rodrigue 2002, 135.
116. Rodrigue 2001, 136–38.
117. Scarpaci 1975, 165.
118. Scarpaci 1975, 165, 172.
119. Scarpaci (1975, 176) indicates that all workers "lived together without any hostility." There were, however, almost certainly isolated issues.
120. Scarpaci 1975, 173–75, 182.
121. Scarpaci 1975, 182.
122. Beechert 1985, 42.
123. Liu 1984, 190; Fleischman and Tyson 2000, 16.
124. Fleischman and Tyson 2000, 16. A similar system used in Australia required two days of labor for one day of missed work (Fleischman and Tyson 2000, 12).
125. Fleischman and Tyson 2000, 16–17.
126. Fleischman and Tyson 2000, 17; Takaki 1983, 74–75; Beechert, 1985, 245.
127. Beechert, 1985, 57.
128. In 1872, 33.4 percent of the accused were acquitted; in 1874 only 28.3 percent were acquitted, dropping to 14.3 percent in 1878 and 13.3 percent in 1880 (Beechert, 1985, 47).
129. Barnes 1964, 83.
130. Liu 1984, 190.
131. Fleischman and Tyson 2000, 12.
132. Fleischman and Tyson 2000, 14.
133. Fleischman and Tyson 2000, 18; Liu 1984, 201.
134. Fleischman and Tyson 2000, 19.
135. Fleischman and Tyson 2000, 19; Beechert 1985, 121.
136. Beechert 1985, 214.
137. Beechert 1985, 18.
138. Kessler 2015, 142–43.
139. Kessler 2015, 130.

140. Beechert 1985, 105.
141. Kessler 2015, 161.

## CHAPTER 2

1. As practiced in Yucatán.
2. As practiced in the Caribbean and Brazil.
3. Alston, Mattiace, and Nonnenmacher 2009; Turner 1911.
4. Williams 2005, 34–35.
5. Williams 2005, 34.
6. Williams 2005, 34–35.
7. Cristine Kray, personal communication, August 28, 2018.
8. Alston, Mattiace, and Nonnenmacher 2009, 104–5; see also Weyl 1902. Fallaw also notes that Simeon Dominguez, owner of the only bar in Mixupip, a village in the henequen zone, would alert hacienda owners when patrons' bar tabs reached twenty to twenty-five pesos. The Hacendado would then offer to assume the debt and allow the patron to work off the debt over time. Few who accepted this offer could ever get out of debt (2002, 43).
9. Meyers and Carlson 2002, 229 (citing Kaerger 1980, 59; Rejón Patrón 1993, 84, 94).
10. Williams 2005, 55.
11. Williams 2005, 34–35; Rugemer 2013, 434.
12. Williams 2005, 55.
13. Lockhart and Schwartz 1983, 219.
14. William quotes British author Richard Ligon as reporting, "Most of the white workers were indentured for five years to repay the cost of their passage, so . . . they have the worser lives, for they are put to very hard labour, ill lodging, and their diet very sleight." Williams also cites British author Richard Ligon's comment, "The slaves and their posterity, being subject to their Masters forever, are kept and preserv'd with greater care than the servants, who are theirs but for five years" (Williams 2005, 33).
15. Renouf et al. 2010, 928.
16. Malik n.d., 15.
17. Asia Farming 2019.
18. This section has been adapted from Gust 2016.
19. Renouf et al. 2010, 928.
20. Renouf et al. 2010, 928.
21. McLeod 2015.
22. As will be discussed in chapter 4, when cane is harvested as piecework, workers are paid by the number of stalks that they cut and dress.
23. Williams 2005, 41.
24. Solomon 2009, 109–10.

25. Solomon 2009, 115.
26. See figures 10 and 11 in Wayne 2010, 27.
27. See Wayne 2010.
28. Williams 2005, 48.
29. Rabelo et al. 2011.
30. Schwartz 1985, 120.
31. The sugar may also be packed into molded and then packed into barrels after the molasses has settled and been drained away.
32. The more refined sugar is, the more molasses is extracted, and the more rum that can be produced from the molasses (Williams 2005, 46–47). Use of full sugarcane for rum was barred in the Leeward Islands from 1644 to 1673, as the island colonies were supposed to produce sugar for export, not rum to keep the locals drunk (Williams 2005, 42).
33. Barty-King and Massel 1983, especially 77–78, 89; Williams 2005, 39, 43.
34. Williams 2005, 46.
35. Williams 2005, 261–62.
36. Williams 2005, 41.
37. Broom 2003, 37; Faria 2003, 349–50; Halliday 2004, 6.
38. Roger Zimmerman, Distillery Master at Richland Rum, personal communication, 2015.
39. The boiling point of alcohol is 78.4°C (Williams 2005, 23) compared to water, which boils at 100°C.
40. Barty-King and Massel 1983.
41. Roger Zimmerman, personal communication, 2015.
42. Owens and Dikty 2009, 31.
43. Wolf and Mintz 1957, 360.
44. In practice, Yucatecan haciendas are intended to be self-contained production and processing facilities. In most cases, one or more cash crops are grown and processed to some degree on-site prior to sale. Exceptions, for example, are salt, which is collected and processed but not produced on-site, and cattle, which are raised on the hacienda but not slaughtered there. The hacienda may have a resident workforce.
45. Scientific name *Agave fourocrydes*, used for making rope and twine.
46. Alexander 2003; Joseph 1986; Joseph et al. 1986; Meyers 2005; Meyers 2012; Wells and Joseph 1996; and Wells 1985.
47. Reed 2001, 10.
48. Alston, Mattiace, and Nonnenmacher 2009; Rugeley 1996; Wells 1985; Mattiace and Nonnenmacher 2014, 372; Raymond 1977, 372; Rivero 1994, 83; Rivero 1999, 30.
49. Rivero 1994, 83; Arnold and Frost 1909, 325; Katz 1980, 19–20; Meyers and Carlson 2002, 228; Turner 1969, 18.

50. Meyers and Carlson 2002, 230; Wells and Joseph 1996, 166; Goveia 1965, 127; Williams 2005, 38.
51. Wells and Joseph 1996, 156.
52. Workers at Xuxub are a notable exception, as discussed later in this chapter.
53. Wells 1985, 24.
54. Taube 2003, 463; see also Re Cruz 1996.
55. In contrast, owners of henequen haciendas and other operations had no limits on how much or what they could export, and produced far more henequen than could be consumed domestically in Yucatán.
56. Mintz 1985, 76; Ambler 2003.
57. Williams 2005, 258.
58. It is unclear whether this man was chosen because he was respected by the workers or because he would brutally enforce discipline. Most likely this varied from farm to farm. See Goveia (1965, 131) for discussion of this under slavery. The capataz, or foreman, appears on labor records from the site of San Eusebio, as discussed in chapter 4.
59. Hall 1971, 7, 60; Rogoziński 1999, 137.
60. Gust 2016, 48; Goveia 1965, 137.
61. Rum, as well as tobacco, was used as a coping mechanism by the enslaved and the indentured alike (Williams 2005, 44). Rum was argued to both help and hurt, justifying its use despite the drawbacks (Williams 2005, 45). See also Berleant-Schiller 1995, 57.
62. Gust 2016, 48; Goveia 1965, 137.
63. Smith 2001, 218–19; Rivero 2003, 572.
64. For the Brazilian case, see Lockhart and Schwartz 1983, 202, 215.
65. Smith 2008, 104–33; Pezzarossi 2017, 158.
66. Goveia 1965, 127; Williams 2005, 38.
67. Williams 2005, 39.
68. Williams 2005, 39.
69. Rogoziński 1999, 114.
70. Rogoziński 1999, 115.
71. Lockhart and Schwartz 1983, 209.
72. Lockhart and Schwartz 1983, 208.
73. Lockhart and Schwartz 1983, 244.
74. For the Brazilian case, see Lockhart and Schwartz 1983, 202, 215.
75. Sheridan 1974, 125–26.
76. Shuler 2005, i.
77. Sheridan 1974, 142.
78. Barnes 1964, 104.
79. Angrosino 2003, 108.
80. Angrosino 2003, 108.

81. Gasnier 1936; Angrosino 2003, 108.
82. Angrosino 2003, 109.
83. Scarpaci 1975, 166.
84. Scarpaci 1975, 169.
85. Scarpaci 1975, 169.
86. Scarpaci 1975, 175.
87. Scarpaci 1975, 165, 172.
88. Scarpaci 1975, 173–75, 182.
89. Barnes 1964, 83.
90. Liu 1984, 186. A total of 45,000 Chinese and 86,400 Japanese laborers were recruited between 1876 and 1900.
91. Fleischman and Tyson 2000, 24; Fuchs, 1961, 115; Daws 1968, 304; Beechert, 1985, 109. Chinese workers were paid at slightly higher rates than Japanese workers (Liu 1984, 205). Fleischman and Tyson 2000, 24.
92. Fleischman and Tyson 2000, 14–15; Fuchs 1961, 146.
93. Liu 1984, 190; Fleischman and Tyson 2000, 16.
94. Fleischman and Tyson 2000, 14–15; Fuchs 1961, 210; Beechert, 1985, 64.
95. Fleischman and Tyson 2000, 25; Takaki, 1983, 75–76.
96. Martinez 1999, 66; see also Plant 1987, 18.
97. Martinez 1999, 73.
98. Alston, Mattiace, and Nonnenmacher 2009, 119, citing personal communication from Pieded Peniche Rivero.
99. Ambler 2003, 74, 77.
100. Smith 2001, 215–17.
101. Smith 2001, 214; see also Vogt 1979, 71, and Curto 1996.
102. Smith 2001, 218.
103. Smith 2001, 218–19.
104. Smith 2001, 221.
105. Smith 2001, 221–22; Gaspar 1985, 244; Craton 1982, 118, 122; Smith 2001, 222, citing Williams 1932, 163; Smith 2001, 222, citing Edwards 1794, 78.
106. Meyers and Carlson 2002, 229; Wells 1985, 158.
107. Alexander 1999, 109; 2003, 192–93.
108. Wells and Joseph 1996, 159.
109. Wells and Joseph 1996; Rivero 1999, 18; 2003, 572.
110. Wells and Joseph 1996, 170, see also Taylor 1979, 43, 64, for the same phenomenon in central México and Oaxaca.
111. Wells and Joseph (1996, 169) report "alcohol probably both augmented and diminished resistance on the henequen estates." Opie (2012, 115) echoes this sentiment for Guatemala.
112. Wells and Joseph 1996, 156–57.

## CHAPTER 3

1. Gibson 1964, 20; see also Daniel 1992, 193.
2. Farriss 1984, 98; Patch 1993, 20.
3. Patch 1985; Rivero 2003; Sweitz 2012b.
4. *Encomenderos* is defined as those granted an encomienda by the Spanish Crown. Lockhart 1969, 414–15; Patch 1993, 20; Sweitz 2012b, 243; see also Rey 1976.
5. Patch 1993, 27; Sweitz 2012b, 243.
6. Patch (1993, 30) indicates that the date for the first repartimiento in Yucatán is unknown but that they were in place by 1617.
7. Brennan 1966; Patch 1993, 33; see also Chapa 1981, 513.
8. This is a variation of *corvée* labor.
9. Patch 1993, 30.
10. Patch 1993, 30.
11. Wolf 1956, 1067.
12. Batchelder and Sanchez 2013, 46.
13. The New Laws of 1542 restricted inheritability to two successive heirs, after which the encomienda would revert to the Crown. In a few impoverished areas, including the Yucatán Peninsula, these laws were relaxed and the encomiendas were regranted again and again to the same family (Patch 1993, 32–33).
14. Chevalier 1970, 299.
15. Farriss 1984, especially 39–40, 78–79, 375.
16. Brackish or freshwater watercourses through mangroves are referred to as *rias* in Yucatán. These are not true rivers (*rios*) that cross dry land, but are both translated into English as "river" (Marco Lazcano-Barrero, personal communication, July 2017).
17. Fedick and Taube 1995; Fedick 1998; Fedick et al. 2000; Gómez-Pompa et al. 2003; Patch 1985, 23; 2003.
18. Patch 2003, 567.
19. Patch 1985, 25–26.
20. Patch 1985, 39.
21. Patch 1993, 119.
22. Patch 1985, 29.
23. Alexander 2004, 2; Patch 1985, 30–31.
24. Patch 1985, 31–32.
25. Patch 1985, 33.
26. Aguardiente is a form of rum.
27. Patch 1985, 34.

28. Patch (1985, 34) does not indicate whether these complaints were due to Campechano planters flooding the sugar market or because they claimed a right to export sugar into Yucatán.

29. The grains produced included maize and rice (Patch 1985, 32, 34–35).

30. Rum production in Cuba fell under the same ban (Gjelten 2008, 18). Thus, while imported legally under Yucatecan law, the rum appears to have been illegally produced.

31. Taylor 1979, 55.

32. Cline 1950 and Manual del Mayordomo 1860 in Rivero 2003, 578.

33. A milpa is a small-scale traditional farm.

34. Patch 1985, 42–43.

35. Patch 1985, 44.

36. Meyers and Carlson 2002, 228; see also Patch 1985, 43; Baerlein 1914, 30; Raymond 1977, 372; Wells 1984, 223.

37. Patch 1985, 43; Rivero 2003, 577–78.

38. Patch 1985, 43.

39. Patch 1985, 44; see also Rivero 2003, 577.

40. Foster 1997, 110; Rodríguez O. 2012, 232–34.

41. Foster 1997, 110–11; Rodríguez O. 2012, 342–45; Cline 1947, 32–34; see also Farriss 1984, 375–88, especially 384–86.

42. This represents a relatively small portion of Yucatán's total area, but good agricultural land is scarce in the Yucatán Peninsula. See Alston, Mattiace, and Nonnenmacher 2009, 110; Sweitz 2012b, 241.

43. Patch 1985, 44.

44. Katz 1974, 4.

45. Reed 2001, 177.

46. Katz 1974, 2; see also Meyers and Carlson 2002, 227.

47. Patch 1985, 44; Rivero 1999; Robinson 2011, 212.

48. Sweitz (2005, 428) disagrees with Patch's (1993, 153) contention that external forces were not involved in the development of the market for sugar and cane alcohol because of the European goods found during excavations of the lowest colonial period strata at Hacienda Tabi. See also Patch 1985, 48; Sweitz 2012b, 241.

49. Florescano 1987, 264.

50. Wells and Joseph 1996, 159.

51. Alston, Mattiace, and Nonnenmacher 2009, 110.

52. Reed 2001, 72.

53. Rugeley 1996, 130.

54. Reed 2001, 67–73; Rugeley 1996, xii; Sullivan 2004.

55. Rugeley 1996, 123.

56. Dumond 1985; Dumond 1997; Reed 2001.

57. Reed 2001, 299–301; Farriss 1984, 19.

58. Patch 1985; Patch 2003.
59. Reed 2001, xi.
60. Reed 2001, especially 134.
61. Reed 2001.
62. Reed 2001, 197; Sullivan 2004.
63. Reed 2001, 197; Sullivan 2004, 36.
64. Sullivan 2004, 28, 36, 52.
65. Meyers and Carlson 2002, 228; Rugeley 2009; Bracamonte y Sosa 1993, 154; Meyers and Carlson 2002, 228–29; Rivero 2003, 577; Wells 1984, 221–22.
66. Henequen is also known as *Agave fourcroydes*.
67. Rivero 2003, 571.
68. Alston, Mattiace, and Nonnenmacher 2009, 112n28.
69. Alston, Mattiace, and Nonnenmacher 2009, 113.
70. Alston, Mattiace, and Nonnenmacher 2009, 109.
71. International Harvester Company was created through the merger of the McCormick Harvesting Machine Company, the Deering Harvester Company, and three small firms in 1902. Prior to that, the former constituent parts of the International Harvester Company held a near monopoly on henequen imports into the United States.
72. Alston, Mattiace, and Nonnenmacher 2009, 109.
73. Alston, Mattiace, and Nonnenmacher 2009, 119–20; Rivero 2003, 572; Sweitz 2012b, 242.
74. Joseph 1986; Joseph et al. 1986; Wells and Joseph 1996.
75. Alston, Mattiace, and Nonnenmacher 2009, 109; Joseph 1986; Joseph 1988, 45–48; Wells and Joseph 1996.
76. Wells and Joseph 1996, 158.
77. Mattiace and Nonnenmacher 2014, 369; Rivero 1999, 7.
78. Wells and Joseph 1996, 96, 101.
79. Wells and Joseph 1996, 101.
80. Alexander 1999, 109; Alexander 2003, 193. Peculiarities of law that regulated when women could control their own finances (only adult women not currently married) resulted in a disproportionate number of lenders being widows loaning in their own right (Levy 2008, especially 436–43).
81. Alexander 1999, 134; Alexander 2003; see also Hunt 1974; Brading 1977; Florescano 1987.
82. Wells and Joseph 1996, 98–99; see also Joseph et al. 1986; Wells 1985.
83. Turner 1911; Alexander 1999; 2003; 2004; 2006; Meyers 2005; 2012; Meyers and Carlson 2002; Meyers, Harvey, and Levithol 2008.
84. Alston, Mattiace, and Nonnenmacher 2009.
85. Katz 1974, 2.
86. A mecate is equal to a square twenty meters on a side—four hundred square meters (Rivero 1999, 26).

87. Bracamonte y Sosa 1993; Brannon and Joseph 1991; Irigoyen Rosado 1980; Joseph 1986; 1988; Katz 1974; Knight 1986; Mattiace and Nonnenmacher 2014; Raymond 1977; Rivero 1998; 1999; 2003; Sullivan 2004; Sweitz 2012b; Turner 1911; Wells 1985; Wells and Joseph 1996; Zavala 1935.
88. Rasping machines are sometimes referred to as scraping or disfibering machines. See Nickel 1997, 71.
89. Knight 1986, 62; Turner 1911, 25.
90. Rejón Patrón 1993, 81–82, in Meyers and Carlson 2002, 230. As discussed in chapter 2, sugar workers were sometimes forced to work up to twenty hours per day during harvest season (Wells and Joseph 1996).
91. Meyers and Carlson 2002, 230; Sweitz 2012b, 243.
92. Knight 1986, 103.
93. Rivero 1999, 5; 2003, 572; Alston, Mattiace, and Nonnenmacher 2009, 119; Mattiace and Nonnenmacher 2014, 388; Meyers and Carlson 2002, 228; Rivero 1999, 5; 2003.
94. Wedding guests expected to be fed and provided with alcoholic drink.
95. Fallaw 2002, 43.
96. Rivero 2003, 572, 581.
97. Rivero 2010, 212.
98. Alston, Mattiace, and Nonnenmacher 2009, 119; Sullivan 1991, 164.
99. Arnold and Frost 1909, 325.
100. Knight 1986, 64.
101. Villanueva Mukul et al. 1990, 82.
102. Meyers and Carlson 2002, 229.
103. Alston, Mattiace, and Nonnenmacher 2009, 106; Mattiace and Nonnenmacher 2014, 367; see also Wells and Joseph 1996, 163.
104. Alston, Mattiace, and Nonnenmacher 2009.
105. Katz 1974, 18; see also Wells 1985, 157.
106. Rivero 1994, 75.
107. Rivero 1994, 81; see also Wells and Joseph 1996, 148.
108. Baerlein 1914, 152; Kaerger 1980, 59; Meyers and Carlson 2002, 228.
109. Rivero 2003, 575.
110. Bracamonte y Sosa 1993, 152; Meyers and Carlson 2002, 229; Tozzer 1907, 37.
111. Rivero 1994, 83.
112. Alston, Mattiace, and Nonnenmacher 2009, 115.
113. Alston, Mattiace, and Nonnenmacher 2009.
114. Rivero 2003, 572. This status, while important for older men, was not likely to induce a man to accept debt peonage when he was young because, presumably, older parents would be cared for by their sons and daughters late in life if not living on the hacienda.

115. Rivero 1994, 83; Alston, Mattiace, and Nonnenmacher 2009, 126.

116. Price lists for company stores have not been found, but Terry (1909, 574) lists ready-to-serve meal prices in Mérida, Yucatán, ranging from 0.40 to 0.75 pesos each, and hotel rooms ranging from 1.5 to 10 pesos per night, with a shower or bath costing an additional 0.5 or 0.75 pesos, respectively (Alston et al. 2009, 126).

117. The Ludlow Collective 2001, 2008.

118. Sweitz 2012b, 247.

119. Wells 1985, 24.

120. Sweitz 2012b, 247.

121. Alston, Mattiace, and Nonnenmacher 2009, 116; Nickel 1997, 171–74, 191.

122. Katz 1974, 42.

123. Meyers and Carlson 2002, 229.

124. Alston, Mattiace, and Nonnenmacher 2009, 132.

125. Joseph 1988; Knight 1986, 103; Turner 1911; Wells and Joseph 1996, 157; Meyers and Carlson 2002, 229.

126. Alston, Mattiace, and Nonnenmacher (2009, 112) report that the normal daily quota was 2,500 and cite Chardon (1960), who reports a quota of 2,000–2,500 leaves cut per day. Wells and Joseph (1996, 169) report a quota of 1,500–2,000 per day (Rivero 1999, 25).

127. Rivero 1999, 25.

128. Rivero 2003, 576; Patch 1985, 35.

129. Meyers and Carlson 2002, 228; see also Mattiace and Nonnenmacher 2014, 383; Joseph 1988, 29; Turner 1911; Wells 1984, 226–27; Joseph 1985, 164–65.

130. Alston, Mattiace, and Nonnenmacher 2009, 119.

131. *Scrip* is used in an inclusive sense. It may be in the form of paper, coins/tokens, or just as credit in the hacienda's or operation's accounts, and is used in lieu of government-issued currency.

132. Meyers and Carlson 2002, 229; Rivero 1999, 30; Wells 1985, 158.

133. Arnold and Frost 1909, 325; Katz 1974, 19–20; Meyers and Carlson 2002; Turner 1911, 18.

134. Katz 1974, 5.

135. For a review of practice and agency theory applied to archaeology, see Dornan 2002. See also Bourdieu 1977; Giddens 1979.

136. Palka 2005.

137. Sullivan 2004, 170; Juárez 1996, especially 54–57.

138. Joyce 2010, 34. De Certeau's (1985) views critique Foucault's views that focus on the totalizing surveillance of the power structure.

139. Meyers 2005, 131.

140. Burning sugarcane fields facilitated harvest by clearing the underbrush but also filled the cane at ground level. The cane then had to be harvested

quickly or it would start to decay. Some West Indian legislatures imposed the death penalty on slaves convicted of setting malicious fires in cane fields (Goveia 1965, 113).

141. Meyers 2012, 1–18.

142. Wells and Joseph 1996, 162.

143. Sullivan 2004, 21.

144. Abbott 2001, 130.

145. Abbott 2001, 132–33.

146. Williams 2005, 54.

147. As a result of the Mexican Revolution of 1910, the revolutionary army gained control of Yucatán in 1914–15. See Alston, Mattiace, and Nonnenmacher 2009, 106n7; Wright 2009, 16; Krauze 1997, 288–304, 446–52.

148. Berleant-Schiller 1995, 58.

149. Hall 1971, 36; Berleant-Shiller 1995, 57.

150. Fallaw 1997, 554.

151. Fallaw 1997, 553; Joseph 1988.

152. Fallaw 1997, 554.

153. Fallaw 1997, 558.

154. *Indigenismo* is defined as pride in and an understanding of one's indigenous cultural heritage (Fallaw 1997, 555, emphasis added).

155. Fallaw 1997, 556.

156. Knight 1980, 31.

157. Knight 1980, 32.

158. Chardon 1963, 176.

159. Chardon 1963, 177.

160. Fallaw 1997, 561.

161. Chardon 1963, 179; see also Wright 2009, 18.

162. Chardon 1963, 177.

163. Fallaw 1997, 577.

164. Chardon 1963, 187, 193; Eastman and Robert 2000; Brannon and Baklanoff 1984, 137–38.

## CHAPTER 4

1. North of the current state of Quintana Roo.

2. Andrews 1985, 140; Edwards 1986, 123–24.

3. Andrews 1985.

4. Chamberlain 1948, 237–52.

5. Andrews 1985, 140; Andrews and Jones 2001; Careaga Viliesid 1990, 34–36; Colinas 1989; Edwards 1986, 124.

6. Apestegui 2002, 192; Edwards 1957, 149–54; Le Plongeon 1889. The logwood tree, also known as dyewood, is species *Haematoxylum campechianum*.

7. Andrews 1985, 140; Pi-Sunyer and Thomas 1999, 6.
8. Breglia 2009, 251–55.
9. Rugeley 1996, xiv, xvi–xvii.
10. Meyers 2012, 39; Reed 2001, 85, 206, 281.
11. Reed 2001, 197.
12. Dumond 1970, 272.
13. Reed 2001, 177; Rugeley 2001, 162–63.
14. Alston, Mattiace, and Nonnenmacher 2009; Rugeley 1996; Wells 1985.
15. Andrews 1985, 140; Sullivan 2004, 52, 97, 120.
16. Solferino may be the site we have identified as Monte Bravo.
17. The history of Xuxub, including the attack in which Robert L. Stephens was killed, is masterfully detailed in Paul Sullivan's book *Xuxub Must Die: The Lost Histories of a Murder on the Yucatán* (2004). Sullivan does not provide a definite date for the founding or purchase of Xuxub but does say that Palmero had founded the operation only two to three years before (Sullivan 2004, 20) and that Ramon Aznar reported his partnership with Robert L. Stephens began in 1872 (Sullivan 2004, 69). Palmero's petition to the Mexican government for vacant land is dated November 15, 1869 (Sullivan 2004, 201n29).
18. Sullivan 2004, 34–35.
19. Sullivan 2004, 16.
20. Sullivan 2004, 21.
21. An *ejido* refers to agricultural lands held communally by a community.
22. Sullivan 2004, 27.
23. In context this is more of an access path or walking trail than a true road.
24. Sullivan 2004, 27–29, 126; see also Sullivan 1998, 57.
25. Reed 2001, 272; Sullivan 1998, 56; 2004, 117.
26. Reed 2001, 272; Sullivan 1998, 60; 2004, 79.
27. Sullivan 2004, 79, 120.
28. Bernardino Cen's skull is on display at the Caste War Museum in Tihosuco, Yucatán.
29. Sullivan 2004, 123.
30. Sullivan 2004, 121, 156, 166.
31. Sullivan 2004, 79, 120.
32. Sullivan 2004, 197–255; Paul Sullivan, personal communication, 2010. Aznar claimed that Stephens was an employee, not a partner; as such, his heirs were not entitled to any proceeds from Xuxub (Sullivan 2004).
33. Gust 2016, 123; Gust and Mathews 2011.
34. Don Vio, personal communication, 2011. Paul Sullivan, personal communication, 2009. This brick noted here may have been used originally as a ship ballast.
35. Wayne 2010, 25–27.

36. Gust 2016, 134; Mathews, Croatt, and Gust n.d.; Mathews and Croatt 2010; 2017.

37. Measuring 4.0 m by 5.0 m and 1.5 m tall.

38. Both wells are both approximately 1.5 m in diameter and each more than 4 m deep. The first well is located slightly northwest of the storage structure, and the second well is located 70 m east of the sugar-refining building.

39. This feature is located 330 m east-southeast of the site architecture.

40. Gust 2016, 196.

41. Sullivan 2004, 22, 247.

42. Surface collection was conducted systematically by Mathews and Gust in 2011, and opportunistically by Gust in 2014 as part of his dissertation fieldwork. Excavation was limited, and four 1 m by 1 m units were excavated in this area.

43. The 2014 surface collections were designated as Operation 22A, and each collection location was numbered sequentially (1–18); 2011 surface collections were designated as Operation 26A during artifact analysis, and each collection location was numbered sequentially (e.g., Op22A/3 or Op26A/12).

44. Eighty-six percent of artifacts were recovered through surface collection.

45. Gust 2016, 169. One hundred and three 30 cm diameter shovel probes were excavated at Xuxub. Shovel probes at Xuxub were designated as Operation 20. Areas probed were given a sequential letter (A–C). Each individual shovel probe was assigned a number. Thus the tenth shovel probe excavated in area B is referred to as Op20B/10. Note that water in the nearby Laguna Yalahau is brackish and unsuitable for consumption.

46. Soil in the shovel probes near the wall (Op20C) was clayey, wet to water-logged during excavation, and smelled, implying that despite original indications, the water table was high regularly or continually in this area, making it unsuitable for housing.

47. A soil sample was collected from each shovel for soil phosphate testing using the Mehlich II method (Eidt 1977; Hutson et al. 2009; Bethell and Máté 1989; Dauncey 1952; Mehlich 1978; Meyers, Harvey, and Levithol 2008; Beach et al. 2006; Parnell, Terry, and Golden 2001; Eidt and Woods 1974; Eidt 1973). Soil sampling from shovel probes at Xuxub was designated Operation 21 and otherwise used the same naming system as shovel probes (i.e., the soil sample from shovel probe Op20B/10 is Op21B/10).

48. Phosphate levels within shovel probes in which artifacts were found were not statistically different from levels within shovel probes that did not contain artifacts (Gust 2016, 186).

49. Sullivan 2004, 254.

50. The use of phosphate testing was experimental. Every other site where this method was used successfully was occupied significantly longer than San Eusebio and Xuxub, had bounding features that organic material could be

piled against, or both. We speculate that poor phosphate results may be due to the short period of occupation and lack of infrastructure, like walls, against which debris is often piled and left to rot.

51. Sullivan 2004, 6; Shovel Probe Op20A/4.

52. These features are located approximately 300 m and 360 m from the standing structures.

53. The ceramics referenced are American- or British-style improved white earthenware.

54. The bottles at Xuxub are of various shapes and sizes, so regardless of their age, it is not likely that they were purchased to be filled with rum made on-site.

55. Lanman and Kemp-Barclay 2017.

56. Case bottle.

57. Fike 1987, color plate 67.

58. Rum produced using only cane juice. Rhum agricole is typically used for such rum produced in French-speaking areas.

59. Lorrain 1968, 42; Newman 1970, 75.

60. Fike 1987, 8–9.

61. Reed 2001, 272; Sullivan 1998, 60; Sullivan 2004, 79.

62. Hobson 2001.

63. Sullivan 2004, 6; Gust 2016, 267.

64. Of the total cultural material, 0.1 percent was collected.

65. Yaeger et al. 2002.

66. Gust 2016, 306.

67. See appendix.

68. This category would include flatware, but we found none.

69. Wells and Joseph (1996, 47) reports the size of the land grant as 200,000 ha. See also Glover 2006, 239; Villalobos González 1993, 91.

70. Wells and Joseph 1996, 52.

71. The size was equivalent to 241,083 ha (Villalobos González 1993, 92; see also González 2014; Wells and Joseph 1996, 45).

72. San Eusebio sits on a mix of San Angel-Chiquila ejido and private land. See also El Hacendado Mexicano y Fabricante de Azucar 1906, 273, 369; 1907, 399; 1908, 9, 129, 249; González 2014; Gust 2016, 87.

73. This feature is approximately 15 m tall and 5 m in diameter.

74. See Wayne 2010, 24–27. The Jamaica Train sugar-processing house is approximately 5.7 m by 9.5 m.

75. This feature is 7 m by 5 m by 4 m.

76. A fourth well is located on a modern private house lot northwest of the smokestack and may have been part of San Eusebio.

77. The presence of a metal fermentation tank that was removed is also a distant possibility.

78. The hole is 0.20 m.

79.   The doorway is 1.5 m by 2.5 m.

80.   The opening is approximately 1.2 m by 1.2 m.

81.   This feature is 22 m from the industrial building.

82.   This discussion of El Cuyo Company labor records is adapted from Gust 2016, chapter 5.

83.   Also known as the Archivo General en Yucatán (AGEY).

84.   González 2014, 269.

85.   See also Gonzales 2014.

86.   Alston, Mattiace, and Nonnenmacher 2009, 119.

87.   A mecanico is more of a millwright than a mechanic.

88.   A 20 m by 20 m area is known as a mecate.

89.   No names that are exclusive to women appear in the labor records. The only name that is gender ambiguous in these documents is Pilar Hernandez.

90.   Alston, Mattiace, and Nonnenmacher 2009, 119, citing personal communication from Pieded Peniche Rivero.

91.   Foreign workers were paid but nameless in the records. Maya women were not paid (or not directly paid) and are nameless in the records.

92.   Sullivan 2004, 1.

93.   Records indicate that there was an El Cuyo finca at Solferino, but it is unclear if this Solferino is the (possibly retasked) sugar operation, or just bears a similar name.

94.   National Oceanic and Atmospheric Administration 2009.

95.   Gust excavated 295 shovel probes at San Eusebio. Shovel probing was designated as Operation 1. Areas probed were given a sequential letter (A–D). Each individual shovel probe was assigned a number. Thus the fifth shovel probe excavated in area C is referred to as Op1C/5. There were eleven 1 m by 1 m units. Two excavation units, Operation 6A and 6B, did not yield historic material and are not discussed here.

96.   Soil sampling from shovel probes at San Eusebio was designated Operation 2 and otherwise used the same naming system as shovel probes (i.e., the soil sample from shovel probe Op1C/5 is Op2C/5). Soil was collected between 5 cm and 15 cm below the surface. A small number of shovel probes reached bedrock at less than 10 cm. In these cases, no soil sample was collected from that shovel probe. See Gust 2016, 187, 195–97.

97.   Excavations near the building doorway were designated Operation 7. Each 1 m by 1 m unit was given a letter (A–B), and each excavation lot was assigned a sequential number. The second lot from unit B is Op7B/2.

98.   These excavation units were designated Operation 5 and utilized the same system as used for Operation 7. Thus these 1 m by 1 m excavation units were designated Op5A–Op5H. Op5F was laid out and assigned a designation, but not excavated.

99.   Yaeger et al. 2002.

100. Density was high enough in this artifact scatter to make a grid-based systematic collection necessary. Artifact collection in this area was designated Operation 5. Each 5 m-by-5 m area was assigned a letter (A–Y). Each lettered area was subdivided into four 2.5 m by 2.5 m areas, and each of these was assigned a number (1–4). This underrepresents the total artifacts present, as due to local concerns, Gust only collected only bases and mouths (finishes) from large beverage-style bottles from Operation 4. Artifact collections from outside the Operation 4 grid were designated as Operation 3, with each artifact location designated as a letter (A–H) and assigned to Lot 1.

101. Lindsey 2010.

102. Lindsey 2010.

103. Lindsey 2010.

104. Based on the modern label for Bálsamo del Dr. Castro as marketed in 2016.

105. The amount of subsistence-related material from Xuxub is itself surprisingly small.

106. There was a total of 7.55 percent at San Eusebio compared to 4.05 percent at Xuxub.

107. Bottle glass makes up 54.7 percent of the site assemblage. Glass attributed to nonalcoholic use makes up 32.8 percent of the assemblage, and alcohol bottle glass is 21.9 percent of the assemblage.

108. Wells and Joseph 1996, 159.

109. Andrews 1985, 140; Reed 2001, 177; Rugeley 2001, 162–63; Reed 2001, 197.

110. Wells and Joseph 1996, 159.

111. Fallaw 2002, 41.

## CHAPTER 5

1. Angrosino 2003, 101; Pezzarossi 2017, 162. See also Taylor (1979, 93) on the connection between drunkenness and domestic violence in central México and Oaxaca.

2. Schwartzkopf 2012, 23.

3. Bruman 1970; Paredes 1975; Mitchell 2004; Pierce and Toxqui 2015.

4. For potential evidence of pre-Hispanic distillation in México, see Zizumbo-Villarreal 2009.

5. Jocote is known as species *Spondias purpurea*, a small fruit to make wine (Bruman 2000, 94–95). Coyol palm is *Acrocomia Mexicana*, used to make wine (Bruman 2000, 87, 90–91). See Schwartzkopf 2012, 22–23.

6. The natural limit of alcohol content in unfermented beverages is approximately 15 percent (Zizumbo-Villarreal et al. 2009, 414).

7. Sampeck and Schwartzkopf 2017a, 1. The agave species used to make pulque in central México are not found in the Maya area, but Maya did make a

form of pulque before and after European contact (Karl Taube, personal communication, February 2018).

8. Taylor 1979, 58. Taylor (1979, 66) indicates that the problems associated with pulque consumption occurred more frequently in unstructured situations (i.e., less often in situations like religious rites).

9. De Barrios 1999, 18.

10. Redfield and Villa-Rojas (1962, 49) report that sugar partially replaced honey in balché in their study of circa 1930 Chan Kom.

11. Chuchiak 2003, 149–50.

12. *Cofradia* is a Spanish term for a religious cofraternity adopted by Maya (Carey 2012a, 127). Maya cofradias became more politically influential after liberal reforms reduced the power of the Roman Catholic Church in Guatemala following the 1871 elections (Garrard-Burnett 2012, 165). Officially, cofradias are voluntary associations of lay persons that are recognized by the Roman Catholic Church and function to do good works in their communities. In this context, cofradias are groups of Maya who applied the idea of this type of fraternal association instead to resist the ban on native religious practice imposed by the church. See also Garrard-Burnett 2012, 170–71.

13. Chuchiak 2003, 142–43.

14. Redfield and Villa Rojas 1962 (originally published in 1934), 131.

15. Karl Taube, personal communication, November 21, 2017. Corn beer is also known to Maya as *boj* when made with cane sugar (Sieder 2000, 297).

16. Schwartzkopf 2012, 20; 2017, 610.

17. Bristol 2017, 131.

18. Toxqui 2014, 108; Taylor 1979, 61.

19. Dunn 2012, 79; Taylor 1979, 53. Carey (2012c, 8) says that approximately 250 pulquerias operated without a license inside México City in 1639.

20. Aykroyd (1967, 88; see also Hatton 2014) reports that rum was first made in Barbados in the 1630s and that sugarcane was imported from Brazil in 1637. If this information is correct, logically it sets the first rum production in or after 1637, as importation of such quantities of sugar into Barbados seems unlikely. Mintz (1985, 44) also discusses rum transport between Britain and its colonies shortly after 1660. Similarly, Schwartzkopf (2017, 64) says aguardiente was probably widely available in highland Guatemala by the mid-seventeenth century.

21. Carey 2012c, 1.

22. Schwartzkopf 2012, 30.

23. Schwartzkopf 2012, 31.

24. Vogt 1969, 141–44.

25. Vogt 1969, 181, 445.

26. Vogt 1969, 197–200.

27. Vogt 1969, 210–11.

28. Vogt 1969.
29. Garrard-Burnett 2012, 164.
30. Carey, 2014, 131.
31. Carey 2012c, 4.
32. As Garriott and Raikhel (2015) discuss, the notion of addiction is extremely complicated and beyond the scope of this book. However, we do believe that in this particular context, those in power encouraged the abuse of alcohol within a population that had previously restricted its use within a ritual context.
33. Schwartzkopf 2017, 66.
34. Carey 2014, 137.
35. Carey 2012c, 14; Opie 2012, 98, 114; Smith 2008, 104–33.
36. Wells and Joseph 1996, 170; see also Taylor (1979, 43, 64) on the same phenomenon in central México and Oaxaca.
37. Meyers and Carlson 2002, 229; Wells 1985, 158.
38. Wells and Joseph 1996, 156.
39. Opie 2012, 97.
40. Opie 2012, 103.
41. Opie 2012, 98.
42. Opie 2012, 99.
43. Opie 2012, 101.
44. Opie 2012, 98.
45. Dunn 2012, 75.
46. Carey 2012c, 10.
47. Dunn 2012, 82; Carey 2012c, 12.
48. Dunn 2012, 83. Opie (2012, 100) argues that women entering vinaterías (and rum shop and taverns) were stigmatized.
49. Dunn 2012, 85. In this context, *aguardiente* refers to grape-based spirits.
50. Toxqui 2017, 104.
51. Toxqui 2014, 109–10.
52. Bristol 2017, 136–37; Pezzarossi 2017, 140.
53. Bristol 2017, 128.
54. Carey 2012c, 10; Opie 2012, 98.
55. Chun Bun Lam, McHale, and Upderaff 2012, 19; Sanchez et al. 2017, 336; Opie 2012, 115.
56. Stross 1967, 59.
57. Ayala, Carrier, and Magaña 1996, 98.
58. Stross 1967, 62.
59. Chun Bun Lam, McHale, and Upderaff 2012, 19; Sanchez et al. 2017, 336.
60. Stross 1967, 65.
61. Stross 1967, 73, 78.
62. Ayala, Carrier, and Magaña 1996, 98.

63. Stross 1967, 63.
64. Stross 1967, 64.
65. Stross 1967, 78.
66. Stross 1967, 71.
67. Ayala, Carrier, and Magaña 1996, 100; Stross 1967, 64.
68. Stross 1967, 71; Ayala, Carrier, and Magaña 1996, 98.
69. Stross 1967, 65.
70. Stross 1967, 73.
71. Stross 1967, 77.
72. Stross 1967, 69, 71.
73. Ayala, Carrier, and Magaña 1996, 98.
74. Ayala, Carrier, and Magaña 1996, 102.
75. Stross 1967, 77.
76. Marrero 2003, 319.
77. De la Cruz Cruz 2003, 294.
78. De la Cruz Cruz 2003, 294; Carey 2012b, 132; 2014, 132; Wells and Joseph 1996, 170.
79. De la Cruz Cruz 2003, 294.
80. Bachrach Ehler 1991, 3.
81. Wells and Joseph 1996, 170.
82. Wells and Joseph 1996, 170. Presumably by "planters," they are referencing hacienda owners or managers.
83. Carey 2014, 132.
84. Fallaw 2002.
85. Fallaw 2002, 41.
86. Fallaw 2002, 42, 49, 51.
87. Fallaw 2002, 49.
88. Fallaw 2002, 46–47.
89. Fallaw 2002, 41; Stern 1999, 379.
90. Stern 1999.
91. Stern 1999, 378; Fallaw 2002, 41.
92. Stern 1999, 382.
93. For further discussion on henequen and hardwood extraction, see, for example, Chardon 1963; Fox 1961; Knight 1986; Napier 1973; Villalobos González 1987; and Wells 1992.
94. Torres and Momsen 2005, 314.
95. Torres and Momsen 2005, 321.
96. Burke Distributing Company, accessed September 15, 2019.
97. Pi-Sunyer and Thomas 2015, 94; Torres 2002a, especially 87–88; Vassallo-Olby 2010, 39; see also Hiernaux-Nicolás 1999, 135.
98. Vassallo-Olby 2010, 39, 42.
99. Clancy 1970, 138; see also Dunning and McQueen 1982, 83; Witt et al. 1991, 61.

100. Andrews 1985, 127; Edwards 1957.
101. Friedlander 1973, 687. Additionally, a study conducted on foreign tourism between 1967 and 1970 demonstrated more than 20 percent annual growth to the nearby island of Cozumel.
102. There was also a resultant mass migration of laborers into the Cancun area (Pi-Sunyer, Thomas, and Daltabuit 1999, 8). See also Alpern 1975, 338; Enriquez Savignac 1972, 108.
103. Clancy 2001, 133; Gormsen 1982, 46, 52.
104. Alpern 1975, 338; Gormsen 1982, 47. This has of course since changed, with direct hits from several hurricanes, including Gilbert in 1988, Wilma in 2005, and Dean in 2007.
105. Enriquez Savignac 1972, 109.
106. Alpern 1975, 338; Gormsen 1982, 47.
107. Enriquez Savignac 1972, 111.
108. Torres 2002a; see also Hiernaux-Nicolás 1999, 138.
109. Torres and Momsen 2004, 303; see also Torres 2000.
110. Dunphy 1972, xxi, 27–28; see also Enriquez Savignac 1972, 110–11.
111. Enriquez Savignac 1972, 111.
112. Alpern 1975, 338.
113. Torres and Momsen 2005, 316–17; Alpern 1975, 338. Migrants moved in from Yucatán, Campeche, México City, Veracruz, and Guererro (Gormsen 1982, 52, 54).
114. Gormsen 1982, 53; Torres and Momsen 2005, 317.
115. Andrews 1985, 141; Pi-Sunyer, Thomas, and Daltabuit 1999, 5.
116. Torres and Momsen 2005, 319.
117. Hiernaux-Nicolás 1999, 131.
118. Hutchinson 1987, 170.
119. Sheller (2009, 196–97) in Manuel-Navarrete and Redclift (2012, 11).
120. Hernandez 2016. This also comports with the personal experience of the authors. The nature of enforcement and exemption from the laws can vary somewhat from year to year.
121. Torres 2002a, 96, 108.
122. Torres 2002a, 105.
123. Torres 2002a, 105.
124. Torres 2002a, 113.
125. Torres 2002a, 93.
126. Collins 1979, 361.
127. Torres and Momsen (2005, 324) is based on data collected in 1997. Pleas (2011) uses the data from Torres and Momsen (2005). Laguna Puls et al. (2013) classified rooms in the Cancun area based on the number of beds in each room and other criteria, but not based on level of luxury (star rating system).

128. Breglia 2009, 251–55.

## CONCLUSION

1. This body of research includes publications on commodities such as bananas (Koppel 2008), sugar (Mintz 1985), and cod (Kurlansky 1998), among many others.
2. Abollado 2000, 17.
3. Patch 1985, 34; 1993, 142.
4. Alston et al. 2009, 110.
5. Reed 2001, 10.
6. Reed 2001, 290, 293–302.
7. Reed 2001, 265.
8. See González 2014; Gust 2016; Sullivan 2004.
9. Reed 2001, 12.
10. Ayala, Carrier, and Magaña 1996, 98; Toxqui 2017, 104.
11. Fallaw 2002, 41.
12. Baud and Ypeij 2009.
13. Breglia 2009.
14. There was also a resultant mass migration of laborers into the Cancun area (Pi-Sunyer, Thomas, and Daltabuit 1999, 8).
15. Torres 2002, 87.
16. Pi-Sunyer et al. 1999, 8.
17. Such as branded vans that ferry workers to and from resorts and a road connecting the Cancun airport and the Hotel Zone.
18. Gilbert et al. 1986; Wells 1986; Wells and Gilbert 1996.

# REFERENCES

Abbott, Elizabeth, *Sugar: A Bittersweet History*. London: Overlook Press, 2011.

Abollado, Francisco L. Jiménez. "Implantación y Evolución de la Encomienda en la Provincia de Tabasco, 1522–1625." *Anuario de Estudios Americanos* 57, no. 1 (2000): 13–39.

Adams, Lisa J. "Cancun Tolerates Annual Invasion." *The Davis Enterprise*, March 15, 2001.

Aguirre, B. E. "Evacuation in Cancun During Hurricane Gilbert." *International Journal of Mass Emergencies and Disasters* 9, no. 1 (1991): 31–45.

Alberro, Solange. "Bebidas Alcohólicas y Sociedad Colonial en México: Un Intento de Interpretación." *Revista Mexicana de Sociología* 51, no. 2 (1989): 349–59.

Alcorn, P. W. "The Chicle Tree (Manilkara Zapota) in Northwest Belize: Natural History, Forest Floristics, and Management." Master's thesis, University of Florida, 1994.

Alexander, Rani T. "Architecture, Haciendas, and Economic Change in Yaxcabá, Yucatán, Mexico." *Ethnohistory (Special Issue: Beyond the Hacienda: Agrarian Relations and Socioeconomic Change in Rural Mesoamerica)* 50 (2003): 191–220.

Alexander, Rani T. "The Emerging World System and Colonial Yucatán: The Archaeology of Core-Periphery Integration, 1780–1847." In *Leadership, Production, and Exchange: World Systems Theory in Practice*, edited by Paul Nick Kardulias, 103–24. Lanham, Md.: Rowman & Littlefield, 1999.

Alexander, Rani T. "Maya Settlement Shifts and Agrarian Ecology in Yucatán, 1800–2000." *Journal of Anthropological Research* 62 (2006): 449–70.

Alexander, Rani T. *Yaxcabá and the Caste War of Yucatán: An Archaeological Perspective*. Albuquerque: University of New Mexico Press, 2004.

Alpern, David. "Cancun: Construction Boots in the Footsteps of Maya Kings." *New York Times*, March 23, 1975.

Alston, Lee J., Shannan Mattiace, and Tomas Nonnenmacher. "Coercion, Culture, and Contracts: Labor and Debt on Henequen Haciendas in Yucatán, Mexico, 1870–1915." *Journal of Economic History* 69 (2009): 104–37.

Ambler, Charles. "Alcohol and the Slave Trade in West Africa, 1400–1850." In *Drugs, Labor, and Colonial Expansion*, edited by William R. Jankowiak and Daniel Bradburd, 73–87. Tucson: University of Arizona Press, 2003.

Andrews, Anthony P. "The Archaeology and History of Northern Quintana Roo." In *Geology and Hydrogeology of the Yucatán and Quaternary Geology of Northeastern Yucatán Peninsula*, edited by C. Ward, A. E. Weidie, and W. Back, 127–43. New Orleans: New Orleans Geological Society, 1985.

Andrews, Anthony P., and Grant D. Jones. "Asentamientos Colonials en la Costa de Quintana Roo." *Temas Antropológicos* 23, no. 1 (2001): 20–35.

Angrosino, Michael V. "Rum and Ganja: Indenture, Drug Foods, Labor, Motivation, and Evolution of the Modern Sugar Industry in Trinidad." In *Drugs, Labor, and Colonial Expansion*, edited by William R. Jankowiak and Daniel Bradburd, 101–16. Tucson: University of Arizona Press, 2003.

Apestegui, Cruz. *Pirates of the Caribbean*. Translated by Richard Lewis Rees. Edison, N.J.: Chartwell Books. 2002.

Arnold, Channing, and Frederick J. Tabor Frost. *The American Egypt: A Record of Travel in Yucatán*. London: Hutchinson & Company, 1909.

Asia Farming. "Sugarcane Cultivation Guide." Accessed September 21, 2019. https://www.asiafarming.com/sugarcane-cultivation.

Ayala, Armida, Joseph Carrier, and Raúl Magaña. "The Underground World of Latina Sex Workers in Cantinas." In *AIDS Crossing Borders: The Spread of HIV Among Migrant Latinos*, edited by Ross Conno, 425–41. Boulder: Westview Press, 1996.

Aykroyd, Wallace Ruddell. *Sweet Malefactor: Sugar, Slavery and Human Society*. London: Heinemann, 1967.

Bachrach Ehlers, Tracy. "Debunking Marianismo: Economic Vulnerability and Survival Strategies Among Guatemalan Wives." *Ethnology* 30 (1991): 1–16.

Baerlein, Henry. *Mexico: The Land of Unrest*. London: Herbert and Daniel, 1914.

"Bálsamo del Dr. Castro." Accessed February 17, 2019. https://www.facebook.com/balsamodeldrcastro/.

Barbosa, Márcio Henrique Pereira, Marcos Deon Vilela Resende, Luiz Antônio dos Santos Dias, Geraldo Veríssimo de Souza Barbosa, Ricardo Augusto de Oliveira, Luiz Alexandre Peternelli, and Edelclaiton Daros. "Genetic

Improvement of Sugar Cane for Bioenergy: The Brazilian Experience in Network Research with Ridesa." *Crop Breeding and Applied Biotechnology* 12, no. SPE (2012): 87–98.

Barnes, Arthur Chapman. *The Sugar Cane.* New York: Interscience Publishers, 1964.

Barty-King, Hugh, and Anton Massel. *Rum, Yesterday and Today.* London: Heinemann, 1983.

Batchelder, Ronald W., and Nicolas Sanchez. "The Encomienda and the Optimizing Imperialist: An Interpretation of Spanish Imperialism in the Americas." *Public Choice* 156, no. 1–2 (2013): 1–16.

Baud, Michiel and Annelou Ypeij. *Cultural Tourism in Latin America: The Politics of Space and Imagery.* Leiden, Netherlands: Brill.

Bayou Rum, "Taste the Spirit of Louisiana." Accessed February 17, 2019. https://bayourum.com.

Beach, T., N. Dunning, S. Luzzadder-Beach, D. E. Cook, and J. Lohse. 2006. "Impacts of the Ancient Maya on Soils and Soil Erosion in the Central Maya Lowlands." *Catena* 65, no. 2 (2006): 166–78. https://doi: 10.1016/j.catena.2005.11.007.

Beechert, Edward. D. *Working in Hawaii: A Labor History.* Honolulu: University of Hawai'i Press, 1985.

Benedict, Linda. "Leaf Rusts: Old and New Threats to Sugarcane," July 8, 2008. Accessed February 17, 2019. https://www.lsuagcenter.com/portals/communications/publications/agmag/archive/2008/spring/leaf-rusts-old-and-new-threats-to-sugarcane.

Berleant-Schiller, Riva. "From Labour to Peasantry in Montserrat after the End of Slavery." In *Small Islands, Large Questions: Society, Culture and Resistance in the Post-Emancipation Caribbean*, edited by Karen Fog Olwig, 53–72. London: Frank Cass, 1995.

Bethell, Philip, and Ian Máté. 1989. "The Use of Soil Phosphate Analysis in Archaeology: A Critique." In *Scientific Analysis in Archaeology and Its Interpretation*, edited by J. Henderson, 1–29. Los Angeles: University of California, Los Angeles Institute of Archaeology, 1989.

Björk, Peter. "Ecotourism from a Conceptual Perspective: An Extended Definition of a Unique Tourism Form." *International Journal of Tourism Research* 2 (2000): 189–202.

Blumenthal, Ralph. "The Hostelries and Beaches of Modern Cancun." *New York Times*, February 20, 1977.

Bolland, O. Nigel. "Systems of Domination After Slavery: The Control of Land and Labor in the British West Indies After 1838." *Comparative Studies in Society and History* 23, no. 4 (1981): 591–619.

Bonilla, Alejandro, and Matilde Mordt. "Turismo y Conflictos Territoriales en el Pacífico de Nicaragua: El Caso de Tola, Más Allá de los Titulares." *Avance de Investigación (Programa Salvadoreno de Investigación Sobre Desarrollo y Medio Ambiente)* 4 (2008): 1–35.

Bourdieu, Pierre. *Outline of a Theory of Practice*. Translated by Richard Nice. Edited by Ernest Gellner, Jack Goody, Stephen Gudeman, Michael Herzfeld, and Jonathan Parry. Vol. 16, Cambridge Studies in Social and Cultural Anthropology. Cambridge: Cambridge University Press, 1977.

Bowen, Sarah. *Divided Spirits: Tequila, Mezcal, and the Politics of Production*. Berkeley: University of California Press, 2015.

Boyd, Monica. "Oriental Immigration: The Experience of the Chinese, Japanese, and Filipino Populations in the United States." *The International Migration Review* 5, no. 1 (1971): 48–61.

Bracamonte y Sosa, Pedro. *Amos y Sirvientes: Las Haciendas de Yucatán 1789–1860*. Mérida: Universidad Autonoma de Yucatán, 1993.

Brading, David A. "The Hacienda as an Investment." In *Haciendas and Plantations in Latin American History*, edited by Robert G. Keith, 135–40. New York: Homes and Meier, 1977.

Brannon, Jeffery, and Eric N. Baklanoff. *Agrarian Reform and Public Enterprise in Mexico: The Political Economy of Yucatán*. Tuscaloosa: University of Alabama Press, 1987.

Brannon, Jeffrey, and Eric N. Baklanoff. "The Political Economy of Agrarian Reform in Yucatán, Mexico." *World Development*, 12, no. 11/12 (1984): 1131–41.

Brannon, Jeffery T., and Gilbert M. Joseph. *Land, Labour, and Capital in Modern Yucatán: Essays in Regional History and Political Economy*. Tuscaloosa: University of Alabama Press, 1991.

Breglia, Lisa. "Hacienda Hotels and Other Ironies of Luxury in Yucatán, Mexico." In *Cultural Tourism in Latin America The Politics of Space and Imagery*, edited by Michiel Baud and Annelou Ypeij, 245–61. Leiden, Netherlands: Brill.

Brennan, Marie George. "Las Casas and the New Laws." *Revista de Historia de América* 61/62 (1966): 23–41.

Brereton, B. "The Experience of Indentureship: 1845–1917." In *Calcutta to Caroni: The East Indians of Trinidad*, edited by J. La Guerre, 25–38. London: Longmans, 1974.

Bristol, Joan. "Health Food and Diabolic Vice: Pulque Discourses in New Spain." In *Substance and Seduction: Ingested Commodities in Early Modern Mesoamerica*, edited by Stacey Schwartzkopf and Kathryn E. Sampeck, 128–46. Austin: University of Texas Press, 2017.

Broom, Dave. *Rum*. San Francisco: Octopus Publishing, 2003.

Boyd, Monica. "Oriental Immigration: The Experience of the Chinese, Japanese, and Filipino Populations in the United States." *The International Migration Review* 5, no. 1 (1971): 48–61.

Bruman, Henry J. *Alcohol in Ancient Mexico.* Salt Lake City: University of Utah Press, 2000.

Bryce, J. H., and Graham G. Stewart, eds. *Distilled Spirits: Tradition and Innovation.* Nottingham: Nottingham University Press, 2004.

Bun Lam, Chun, Susan M. McHale, and Kimberly A. Updegraff. "Gender Dynamics in Mexican American Families: Connecting Mothers', Fathers', and Youths' Experiences." *Sex Roles* 67 (2012): 17–28.

Burke Distributing Company. "Casa D'Aristi Liqueurs." Accessed September 15, 2019. http://www.burkedist.com/all-products/wine-spirits/kalani-coconut-rum-liqueur#.

Caetano, Raul, Catherine L. Clark, and Tammy Tam. "Alcohol Consumption Among Racial/Ethnic Minorities: Theory and Research." *Alcohol Research and Health* 22, no. 4 (1998): 233–42.

Campari Group. "Wray and Nephew." Accessed February 17, 2019. https://www.camparigroup.com/en/brands/rum/wray-and-nephew.

Careaga Viliesid, Lorena. *Quintana Roo: Una Historia Compartida.* México, Distrito Federal: Instituto de Investigaciones Dr. José María Luis Mora, 1990.

Carey, David, Jr., ed. *Distilling the Influence of Alcohol: Aguardiente in Guatemalan History.* Gainesville: University Press of Florida, 2012.

Carey, David, Jr. "Distilling Perceptions of Crime: Maya Moonshiners and the State, 1898–1944." In *Distilling the Influence of Alcohol: Aguardiente in Guatemalan History,* edited by David Carey Jr., 120–56. Gainesville: University Press of Florida, 2012.

Carey, David, Jr. "Drunks and Dictators." In *Alcohol in Latin America: A Social and Cultural History,* edited by Gretchen Pierce and Áurea Toxqui, 131–58. Tucson: University of Arizona Press, 2014.

Carey, David, Jr. "Introduction: Writing a History of Alcohol in Guatemala." In *Distilling the Influence of Alcohol: Aguardiente in Guatemalan History,* edited by David Carey Jr., 1–16. Gainesville: University Press of Florida, 2012.

Carter, M. *Voices from Indenture: Experiences of Indian Migrants in the British Empire.* New York: Leicester University Press, 1966.

Cater, Erlet. 1995 "Environmental Contradictions in Sustainable Tourism." *The Geographical Journal* 161, no. 1 (1995): 21–28.

Celaya, R., and E. Owen, eds. *Let's Go: The Budget Guide to Mexico.* New York: St. Martin's Press, 1993.

Chamberlain, R. S. *The Conquest and Colonization of Yucatán.* Washington, D.C.: Lord Baltimore Press, 1948.

Chapa, Jorge. "Wage Labor in the Periphery: Silver Mining in Colonial Mexico." *Review (Fernand Braudel Center)* 4, no. 3 (1981): 509–34.

Chardon, Roland. "Hacienda and Ejido in Yucatán: The Example of Santa Ana Cuca." *Annals of the Association of American Geographers* 53, no. 2 (1963): 174–93.

Chardon, Roland Emanuel Paul. 1961. "Some Geographic Aspects of Plantation Agriculture in Yucatán." PhD thesis, University of Minnesota, 1961.

Chevalier, Francois. *Land and Society in Colonial Mexico: The Great Hacienda*. Oakland: University of California Press, 1970.

Chuchiak, John F. "'It Is Their Drinking That Hinders Them': Balché and the Use of Ritual Intoxicants Among the Colonial Yucatec Maya, 1550–1780." *Estudios de Cultura Maya* 24 (2003): 137–71.

Clancy, Michael. "Mexican Tourism: Export Growth and Structural Change Since 1970." *Latin American Research Review* 36, no. 1 (2001): 128–50.

Cline, Harry. "Sugarcane: California's Triple Threat?" *Western Farm Press*, June 20, 2001. Accessed February 17, 2019. http://www.westernfarmpress.com/sugarcane-californias-triple-threat.

Cline, Howard F. "'The Aurora Yucateca' and the Spirit of Enterprise in Yucatán, 1821–1847." *The Hispanic American Historical Review* 27, no. 1 (1947): 30–60.

Cline, Howard F. *Regionalism and Society in Yucatán, 1825–1847: A Study in "Progressivism" and the Origins of the Caste War*. Microfilms Collection of Manuscripts on Middle American Cultural Anthropology, no. 32, University of Chicago, 1950.

Collins, Charles O. "Site and Situation Strategy in Tourism Planning: A Mexican Case Study." *Annals of Tourism Research* 6, no. 3 (1979): 351–66.

Colunga-Garcia Marin, P., and D. Zizumbo-Villarreal. "Tequila and Other Agave Spirits from West-Central Mexico: Current Germplasm Diversity, Conservation and Origin." *Biodiversity and Conservation* 16, no. 6 (June 2007): 1653–67.

Córdoba Azcárate, Matilde. "'Thank God This Is Not Cancun!' Alternative Tourism Imaginaries in Yucatán (Mexico)." *Journal of Tourism and Cultural Change* 9, no. 3 (2011): 183–200.

Crist, Raymond E., and Louis A. Paganini. "Pyramids, Derricks and Mule Teams in the Yucatán Peninsula: A Second Effort in 2,500 Years to Develop a Jungle and Forest Area." *American Journal of Economics and Sociology* 39, no. 3 (1980): 217–26.

Curto, J. C. "Alcohol and Slaves: The Lusa-Brazilian Alcohol Commerce at Mpinda, Luanda, and Benguela During the Atlantic Slave Trade c. 1480–1830 and Its Impact on the Societies of West Central Africa." PhD thesis, University of California, Los Angeles, 1996.

Daniel, Douglas A. 1992. "Tactical Factors in the Spanish Conquest of the Aztecs." *Anthropological Quarterly* 65, no. 4 (1992): 187–94.

Dauncey, K. D. M. "Phosphate Content of Soils on Archaeological Sites." *Advancement of Science* 9, no. 33 (1952): 33–37.

Daws, G. *Shoal of Time: A History of the Hawaiian Islands*. Honolulu: University of Hawai'i Press, 1968.

De Barrios, Virginia B. *A Guide to Tequila, Mezcal and Pulque*. México, Distrito Federal: Minutiae Mexican, 1999.

De Certeau, Michel. *The Practice of Everyday Life.* Berkeley: University of California Press, 1984.

De la Cruz Cruz, Petrona. "A Desperate Woman: A Play in Two Acts." In *Holy Terrors: Latin American Women Perform,* edited by Diana Taylor and Roselyn Costantino, 290–310. Durham: Duke University Press, 2003.

Deerr, Noel. *The History of Sugar.* London: Chapman and Hall, 1949.

Delta Farm Press. "USDA: Katrina Crop Damage at $900 Million." May 15, 2018. Accessed February 17, 2019. http://www.deltafarmpress.com/usda/usda-crop-progress-corn-crosses-halfway-mark-and-then-some.

Diageo. "Brand Introduction." Accessed February 17, 2019. https://www.diageo.com/en/our-brands/brand-introduction/.

Dornan, Jennifer L. "Agency and Archaeology: Past, Present, and Future Directions." *Journal of Archaeological Method and Theory* 9, no. 4 (2002): 303–29.

Dornan, Jennifer L. "'Even by Night We Only Become Aware They Are Killing Us': Agency, Identity, and Intentionality at San Pedro Belize (1857–1930)." PhD thesis, University of California, Los Angeles, 2004.

Dumond, Don E. "Competition, Cooperation, and the Folk Society." *Southwestern Journal of Anthropology* 26, no. 3 (1970): 261–86.

Dumond, Don E. 1997. *The Machete and the Cross: Campesino Rebellion in Yucatán.* Norman: University of Nebraska Press, 1997.

Dumond, Don E. 1985. "The Talking Crosses of Yucatán: A New Look at Their History." *Ethnohistory* 32 (1985): 291–308.

Dunn, Alvis E. "A Sponge Soaking Up All the Money: Alcohol, Taverns, Vinaterias, and the Bourbon Reforms in Mid-Eighteenth-Century Santiago de los Caballeros, Guatemala." In *Distilling the Influence of Alcohol: Aguardiente in Guatemalan History,* edited by David Carey Jr., 71–95. Gainesville: University Press of Florida, 2012.

Dunning, John H., and Matthew McQueen. "Multinational Corporations in the International Hotel Industry." *Annals of Tourism* 9 (1982): 69–90.

Dunphy, Robert J. "Why the Computer Chose Cancun." *New York Times,* March 5, 1972.

Eastmond, A., and M. L. Robert. "Henequen and the Challenge of Sustainable Development in Yucatán, Mexico." *Biotechnology and Development Monitor* 41 (2000): 11–15.

Edwards, Clinton R. "The Human Impact on the Forest in Quintana Roo, Mexico." *Journal of Forest History* 30, no. 3 (1986): 120–27.

Edwards, Clinton R. 1957. "Quintana Roo, Mexico's Empty Quarter." Master's thesis, University of California, Berkeley, 1957.

Egan, Timothy. "Uneasy Being Green: Tourism Runs Wild." *New York Times,* May 20, 2001.

Ehlers, Cindy L. "Variations in Adh and Aldh in Southwest California Indians." *Alcohol Research and Health* 30, no. 1 (2007): 14–17.

Eidt, Robert C. 1977. "Detection and Examination of Anthrosols by Phosphate Analysis." *Science* 197 (1977): 1327–33.

Eidt, Robert C. "A Rapid Chemical Field Test for Archaeological Site Surveying." *American Antiquity* 38 (1973): 206–10.

Eidt, Robert C., and William I. Woods. *Abandoned Settlement Analysis: Theory and Practice.* Shorewood, Wis.: Field Test Associates, 1974.

El Hacendado Mexicano y Fabricante de Azucar. "Advertisement." *El Hacendado Mexicano y Fabricante de Azucar* (12), incomplete, 1906.

El Hacendado Mexicano y Fabricante de Azucar. "Advertisement." *El Hacendado Mexicano y Fabricante de Azucar* (13), incomplete, 1907.

El Hacendado Mexicano y Fabricante de Azucar. "Advertisement." *El Hacendado Mexicano y Fabricante de Azucar* (14), incomplete, 1908.

Enriquez Savignac, Antonio. "The Computer Planning and Coordination of Cancun Island, Mexico: A New Resort Complex." Paper presented at the Third Annual Conference of the Travel Research Association, Quebec, Canada, August 13–16, 1972.

Evans, G. C. "Sugar Manufacture." Paper presented at the Meetings of the Midland Counties Section, Held at the Queen's Hotel, Birmingham, UK, May 15, 1919.

Fallaw, Ben W. "Cárdenas and the Caste War That Wasn't: State Power and Indigenismo in Post-Revolutionary Yucatán." *The Americas* 53, no. 4 (1997): 551–77.

Fallaw, Ben W. "Dry Law, Wet Politics: Drinking and Prohibition in Post-Revolutionary Yucatán, 1915–1935." *Latin American Research Review* 37, no. 2 (2002): 37–64.

Faria, J. B. "Sugar Cane Spirits." In *Fermented Beverage Production*, edited by J. R. Piggott, 348–58. New York: Kluwer Academic / Plenum Publishers, 2003.

Faries, Dave. "Handle The Proof: Which Liquors Burn?" *Dallas Observer*, October 16, 2009. Accessed February 17, 2019. http://www.dallasobserver.com/restaurants/handle-the-proof-which-liquors-burn-7020682.

Farriss, Nancy M. *Maya Society Under Colonial Rule: The Collective Enterprise of Survival.* Princeton, N.J.: Princeton University Press, 1984.

Faust, Betty Bernice. "Maya Environmental Successes and Failures in the Yucatán Peninsula." *Environmental Science and Policy* 4 (2001): 153–69.

Fedick, Scott L. "Ancient Maya Use of Wetlands in Northern Quintana Roo, Mexico." In *Hidden Dimensions: The Cultural Significance of Wetland Archaeology*, edited by Kathryn Bernick, 107–29. Vancouver: University of British Columbia Press, 1998.

Fedick, Scott L., Bethany A. Morrison, Bente Juhl Andersen, Sylviane Boucher, Jorge Ceja Acosta, and Jennifer P. Mathews. 2000. "Wetland Manipulation in the Yalahau Region of the Northern Maya Lowlands." *Journal of Field Archaeology* 27 (2000): 131–52.

Fedick, Scott L., and Karl A. Taube. *The View from Yalahau: 1993 Archaeological Investigations in Northern Quintana Roo, Mexico*. Riverside: University of California, Riverside, 1995.

Fike, Richard E. *The Bottle Book: A Comprehensive Guide to Historic, Embossed, Medicine Bottles*. Salt Lake City: Peregrine Smith Books, 1987.

Finney, Ben R., and Karen Ann Watson, eds. *A New Kind of Sugar: Tourism in the Pacific*. Honolulu: East-West Center, 1977.

Fleischman, Richard K., and Thomas N. Tyson. "The Interface of Race and Accounting: The Case of Hawaiian Sugar Plantations, 1835–1920." *Accounting History* 5, no. 1 (2000): 7–32.

Florescano, E. "The Hacienda in New Spain." In *Colonial Spanish America*, edited by L. Bethell, 250–85. Cambridge: Cambridge University Press, 1987.

FONATUR. "Cancún: El Destino Turístico Mexicano Más Reconocido a Nivel Mundial." Accessed February 19, 2019. http://www.fonatur.gob.mx/es/proyectos_desarrollos/cancun/index.asp.

Ford, Henry, and Samuel Crowther. *My Life and Work*. Garden City, N.Y.: Garden City Publishing, 1922.

Forero, Oscar A., and Michael R. Redclift. "The Role of the Mexican State in the Development of Chicle Extraction in Yucatán, and the Continuing Importance of Coyotaje." *Journal of Latin American Studies* 38 (2006): 61–93.

Forster, Robert. "A Sugar Plantation on Saint-Domingue in the Eighteenth-Century: White Attitudes Towards the Slave Trade." *Historia y Sociedad* (1988): 9–38.

Foss, Richard. *Rum: A Global History*. London: Reaktion Books, 2012.

Foster, Lynn V. *A Brief History of Mexico*. New York: Facts on File, 1997.

Foucault, Michel. "Two Lectures." In *Power/Knowledge*, edited by Colin Gordon, 78–108. New York: Pantheon Books, 1980.

Fox, David A. "Henequen in Yucatán: A Mexican Fibre Crop." *Transactions and Papers (Institute of British Geographers)* 29 (1961): 215–29.

Friedlander, Paul J. C. "Two Vast Projects Sprout in México." *New York Times*, December 2, 1973.

Fuchs, L. H. *Hawaii Pono: A Social History*. San Diego: Harcourt Brace Jovanovich, 1961.

Galloway, Joey. *The Sugar Cane History: An Historical Geography from Its Origin to 1914*. Cambridge: Cambridge University Press, 1989.

Garner, Paul. *Porfirio Díaz: Profiles in Power*. New York: Routledge, 2014.

Garrard-Burnett, Virginia. "Conclusion: Community Drunkenness and Control in Guatemala." In *Distilling the Influence of Alcohol: Aguardiente in Guatemalan History*, edited by David Carey, 157–77. Gainesville: University Press of Florida, 2012.

Garriott, William, and Eugene Raikhel. "Addiction in the Making." *Annual Review of Anthropology* 44 (2015): 477–91.

Gasnier, Louis, dir. *Reefer Madness*. Los Angeles: United Artists Video, 1936.

Gautreaux, Craig. "Louisiana: Sugarcane Crop Poised to Break Record." December 19, 2017. Accessed February 17, 2019. https://agfax.com/2017/12/19/louisiana-sugarcane-crop-poised-to-break-record/.

Gianecchini, J. "Ecotourism: New Partners, New Relationships." *Conservation Biology* 7, (1993): 429–32.

Gibson, Charles. *The Aztecs Under Spanish Rule: A History of the Indians of the Valley of Mexico, 1519–1810*. Stanford: Stanford University Press, 1964.

Giddens, Anthony. *Central Problems in Social Theory*. Berkeley: University of California Press, 1979.

Gjelten, Tom. *Bacardi and the Long Fight for Cuba: The Biography of a Cause*. New York: Viking, 2008.

Glover, Jeffrey B. "The Yalahau Regional Settlement Pattern Survey: A Study of Ancient Maya Social Organization in Northern Quintana Roo, México." PhD thesis, University of California, Riverside, 2006.

Gómez-Pompa, Arturo., Michael F. Allen, Scott L. Fedick, and Juan José Jimenez-Osornio, eds. *The Lowland Maya Area: Three Millennia at the Human-Wildland Interface*. New York: Food Products Press, 2003.

González, Edgar Joel Rangel. "Compañías Deslindadoras y Sociedades Forestales: Empresariado en el Entorno Fronterizo de la Costa Oriental y Creación de un Borde en las Márgenes del Río Hondo, 1876–1935." PhD thesis, Centro de Investigaciones y Estudios Superiores en Antropologia Social, 2014.

Gormsen, E. "Tourism as a Development Factor in Tropical Countries—A Case Study of Cancun." *Applied Geography and Development* 19 (1982): 46–63.

Goveia, Elsa V. *Slave Society in the British Leeward Islands at the End of the Eighteenth Century*. New Haven: Yale University Press, 1965.

Greenleaf Whittier, John. "A Song of Harvest." In *The Writings of John Greenleaf Whittier*. Vol. 4, *Personal Poems, Occasional Poems, The Tent on the Beach*. Boston: Adamant Media, 2001.

Grupo Telles. "História." Accessed February 17, 2019. http://www.grupotelles.com/historia.

Gust, John R. "Bittersweet: Porfirian Sugar and Rum Production in Northeastern Yucatán." PhD thesis, University of California, Riverside, 2016.

Gust, John R., and Jennifer P. Mathews. "Dyewood, Sugar, Rum, and Piracy: The Historic Period of the Costa Escondida, Quintana Roo Mexico." Paper presented at the 110th Meeting of the American Anthropological Association, Montreal, Quebec, 2011.

Hagelberg, Gerhard B. *Sugar in the Caribbean: Turning Sunshine into Money*. Washington, D.C.: Woodrow Wilson International Center for Scholars, 1985.

Hale, Charles A. 1989. "Lucas Alamán, Mexican Conservative." In *The Independence of Mexico and the Creation of the New Nation*, edited by Jaime E. Rodríguez O., 128–34. Los Angeles: University of California, Los Angeles Latin American Center Publications, 1989.

Hall, Douglas. *Five of the Leewards, 1834–1870: The Major Problems of the Post-Emancipation Period in Antigua, Barbuda, Montserrat, Nevis, and St. Kitts.* London: Ginn & Company, 1971.

Halliday, D. J. "Tradition and Innovation in the Scotch Whisky Industry." In *Distilled Spirits: Tradition and Innovation*, edited by J. H. Bryce and Graham G. Stewart, 1–12. Nottingham: Nottingham University Press, 2004.

Hatton, Michael. "The Mark of Cane: A Microeconomic Case Study of Profitability, Accounting and Plantation Management on Three Barbadian Sugar Plantations, 1763–1815." Master's thesis, Dalhousie University, 2014.

Heitmann, John Alfred. *The Modernization of the Louisiana Sugar Industry, 1830–1910.* Baton Rouge: Louisiana State University Press, 1987.

Hernandez, Claudia. "No Alcohol Sales During Weekend Election." *Riviera Maya News,* June 3, 2016.

Hiernaux-Nicolás, Daniel. "Cancún Bliss." In *The Tourist City*, edited by Dennis R. Judd and Susan S. Fainstein, 124–39. New Haven: Yale University Press, 1999.

Hobson, Vincent H., with Melvin Mann. 2001. *Historic and Obsolete Roofing Tile: Preserving the History of Roofing Tiles.* Evergreen, Colo.: Remai Publishing, 2001.

Huffington Post. 2012. "Captain Morgan's Treasure Discovered Near Panama by Captain Morgan–Funded Team." *Huffington Post*, updated December 6, 2017. Accessed February 17, 2019. https://www.huffingtonpost.com/2012/08/01/captain-morgans-treasure_n_1728340.html.

Hunt, Marta Espejo-Ponce. "Colonial Yucatán: Town and Region in the Seventeenth Century." PhD thesis, University of California, Los Angeles, 1974.

Hutchinson, Steven. "Mapping Utopias." *Modern Philology* 85, no. 2 (1987): 170–85.

Hutson, Scott R., Aline Magnoni, Timothy Beach, Richard E. Terry, Bruce H. Dahlin, and Mary Jo Schabel. "Phosphate Fractionation and Spatial Patterning in Ancient Ruins: A Case Study from Yucatán." *Catena* 78 (2009): 260–69.

Inamete, Ufot B. 2014 "Strategic Management and Multinational Corporations: A Case Study of Bacardi." *Global Business Review*, 15, no. 2 (2014): 397–417.

Irigoyen Rosado, Renán. "La Economía de Yucatán Anterior al Auge Henequenero." In *Enciclopedia Yucatánense*, 317–44. Mérida: Edición Oficial del Gobierno de Yucatán, 1980.

Johnson, Frederick I. "Sugar in Brazil: Policy and Production." *Journal of Developing Areas* 17, no. 2 (1983): 243–56.

Joseph, Gilbert M. "From Caste War to Class War: The Historiography of Modern Yucatán (c. 1750–1940)." *The Hispanic American Historical Review* 65, no. 1 (1985): 111–34.

Joseph, Gilbert M. *Rediscovering the Past at Mexico's Periphery: Essays on the History of Modern Yucatán.* Tuscaloosa: University of Alabama Press, 1986.

Joseph, Gilbert M. *Revolution from Without: Yucatán, Mexico, and the United States, 1880–1924.* Vol. 42. Durham, N.C.: Duke University Press, 1988.

Joseph, Gilbert M., Allen Wells, Jeffery T. Brannon, Eric N. Baklanoff, Fred V. Carstensen, and Diane Roazen-Parrillo. *Yucatán y la International Harvester.* Translated by Donna Mellen Webking. Mérida: Maldonado Editores, 1986.

Kaerger, Karl. "Yucatán." In *La Servidumbre Agraria en México en la Época Porfiriana,* edited by Friedrich Katz, 59–60. México, Distrito Federal: Ediciones Era, 1980.

Katz, Friedrich. "Labor Conditions on Haciendas in Porfirian Mexico: Some Trends and Tendencies." *Hispanic American Historical Review* 54 (1974): 1–47.

Katz, Friedrich. *La Servidumbre Agraria en México en la Época Porfiriana,* Vol. 11. México, Distrito Federal: Ediciones Era, 1980.

Kent, Noel. "A New Kind of Sugar." In *A New Kind of Sugar: Tourism in the Pacific,* edited by Ben R. Finney and Karen Ann Watson, 169–98. Honolulu: East-West Center, 1977.

Kessler, Lawrence H. "A Plantation Upon a Hill; or, Sugar Without Rum: Hawai'i's Missionaries and the Founding of the Sugarcane Plantation System." *Pacific Historical Review* 84, no. 2 (2015): 129–62.

Kidd, Vernon. "New Ports of Call in the Caribbean." *New York Times,* September 12, 1982.

Knight, Alan. "Mexican Peonage: What Was It and Why Was It?" *Journal of Latin American Studies* 18 (1986): 41–74.

Knight, Alan. "The Mexican Revolution." *History Today* 30, no. 5 (1980): 28–33.

Krauze, Enrique. *Mexico: A Biography of Power—A History of Modern Mexico, 1810–1996.* New York: Harper Collins, 1997.

Lagunas Puls, Sergio, Ricardo Sonda de la Rosa, Miguel Angel Olivares Urbina, and Natascha Tamara Post. "Analysis of the Room Supply in the Hotel Zone of Cancun, Mexico: Emu 9." *Journal of Tourism Research and Hospitality* 2, no. 2 (2013): 1–8.

Lanman & Kemp-Barclay. 2017. "Famous for Its Many Uses." Last updated June 4, 2017, accessed February 17, 2019. http://floridawater1808.com/index.php?route=pavblog/blog&id=10.

LePlongeon, Alice Dixon. *Here and There in Yucatán: Miscellanies.* New York: J. W. Lovell, 1889.

Linden, Christopher H., and Jeffrey R. Tucker. "Alcoholic Beverages: Proof and Flammability." *The American Journal of Emergency Medicine* 16, no. 5 (1998): 544–45. https://doi.org/10.1016/S0735-6757(98)90016-X.

Lindsey, Bill. 2010. "Historic Glass Bottle Identification and Information Website." Society for Historical Archaeology and Bureau of Land Management. Accessed April 18, 2018 https://sha.org/bottle/.

Liu, John M. "Race, Ethnicity, and the Sugar Plantation System: Asian Labor in Hawaii, 1850–1900." In *Labor Immigration Under Capitalism: Asian Workers in the United States Before World War II*, edited by Lucie Cheng and Edna Bonacich, 186–210. Berkeley: University of California Press, 1984.

Livi-Bacci, Massimo. "The Depopulation of Hispanic America After the Conquest." *Population and Development Review* 32, no. 2 (2006): 199–232.

Livingstone, F. B. "Anthropological Implications of Sickle-Cell Distribution in West Africa." *American Anthropologist* 60 (1958): 533–62.

Lockhart, James. "Encomienda and Hacienda: The Evolution of the Great Estate in the Spanish Indies." *Hispanic American Historical Review* 49 (1969): 411–29.

Lockhart, James, and Stuart B. Schwartz. *Early Latin America: A History of Colonial Spanish America and Brazil*. Cambridge: Cambridge University Press, 1983.

Lorrain, Dessamae. "An Archaeologist's Guide to Nineteenth Century American Glass." *Historical Archaeology* 2 (1968): 35–44.

Louisiana Libations. "Louisiana Distillery Trail." 2018. Accessed February 17, 2019. http://www.libations.louisianatravel.com/distilleries.

The Ludlow Collective. "Archaeology of the Colorado Coal Field War, 1913–1914." In *Archaeologies of the Contemporary Past*, 94–107. London: Routledge, 2001.

The Ludlow Collective. "Ludlow." In *Archaeology as Political Action*, edited by Randall H. McGuire. Berkeley: University of California Press, 2008.

Manual del Mayordomo. *Calendario de Espinosa*. Mérida: Imprenta del Autor, 1860.

Manuel-Navarrete, David, and Michael Redclift. "Spaces of Consumerism and the Consumption of Space: Tourism and Social Exclusion in the 'Mayan Riviera.'" In *Consumer Culture in Latin America*, 177–93. New York: Macmillan Press, 2012.

Manulele Distilleries. "Kō Hana Hawaiian Agricole Rum." Accessed February 17, 2019. https://www.kohanarum.com/home/.

Marrero, Teresa. "Eso sí Pasa Aquí: Indigenous Women Performing Revolutions in Mayan Chiapas." In *Holy Terrors: Latin American Women Perform*, edited by Diana Taylor and Roselyn Costantino, 311–30. Durham, N.C.: Duke University Press, 2003.

Martinez, Samuel. "From Hidden Hand to Heavy Hand: Sugar, the State, and Migrant Labor in Haiti and the Dominican Republic." *Latin American Research Review* 34, no. 1 (1999): 57–84.

Master of Malt. "Dominican Rum." Accessed February 17, 2019. http://www.masterofmalt.com/country/dominican-rum/.

Mathews, Jennifer P., with Gillian P. Schultz. *Chicle: The Gum of the Americas— From the Ancient Maya to William Wrigley*. Tucson: University of Arizona Press, 2009.

Mathews, Jennifer P., and John R. Gust. "Cosmopolitan Living? Examining the Sugar and Rum Industry of the Costa Escondida, Quintana Roo Mexico." In

*The Value of Things: Commodities in the Maya Region from Prehistoric to Contemporary*, edited by Jennifer P. Mathews and Thomas Guderjan, 144–62. Tucson: University of Arizona Press, 2017.

Mathews, Jennifer P., and Stephanie Croatt. "Coastal Commodities: Extractive Industries of the Late Nineteenth and Early Twentieth Centuries in Northern Quintana Roo, Mexico." Paper presented at the SHA 2010 Conference on Historical and Underwater Archaeology, Jacksonville, Florida, 2010.

Mathews, Jennifer P., Stephanie Croatt, and John R. Gust. "Artículos de Costa: Las Industrias Extractivas de Fines del Siglo XIX y Principios del Siglo XX en el Norte de Quintana Roo, México." In *Los Maya de Ayer y Hoy: Memorias del Segundo Congreso Internacional de Cultural Maya, Mexico City*. Forthcoming.

Mattiace, Shannan, and Tomas Nonnenmacher. "The Organization of Hacienda Labor During the Mexican Revolution: Evidence from Yucatán." *Mexican Studies/Estudios Mexicanos* 30, (2014): 366–96.

Mehlich, A. "New Extractant for Soil Test Evaluation of Phosphorus, Potassium, Magnesium, Calcium, Sodium, Manganese and Zinc." *Communications in Soil Science and Plant Analysis* 9 (1978): 477–92.

Meyer-Arendt, Klaus J. "The Costa Maya: Evolution of a Touristic Landscape." *Études Caribéennes: Le Tourisme en Amérique Latine: Enjeux et Perspectives de Développement* 13–14 (2009): paragraphs 1–26.

Meyers, Allan D. 2005. "Material Expressions of Social Inequality on a Porfirian Sugar Hacienda in Yucatán, Mexico." *Historical Archaeology* 39, no. 4 (2005): 112–37.

Meyers, Allan D. *Outside the Hacienda Walls: The Archaeology of Plantation Peonage in Nineteenth-Century Yucatán*. Tucson: University of Arizona Press, 2012.

Meyers, Allan D., Allison S. Harvey, and Sarah A. Levithol. 2008. "Houselot Refuse Disposal and Geochemistry at a Late 19th Century Hacienda Village in Yucatán, Mexico." *Journal of Field Archaeology* 33 (2008): 371–88.

Meyers, Allan D., and David L. Carlson. 2002. "Peonage, Power Relations, and the Built Environment at Hacienda Tabi, Yucatán, Mexico." *International Journal of Historical Archaeology* 6 (2002): 225–52.

Miller, Joseph C. "The Numbers, Origins, and Destinations of Slaves in the Eighteenth-Century Angolan Slave Trade." *Social Science History* 13, no. 4 (1989): 381–419.

Mintz, Sidney W. "Can Haiti Change?" *Foreign Affairs* 74, no. 1 (1995): 73–86.

Mintz, Sidney W. *Sweetness and Power: The Place of Sugar in Modern History*. New York: Penguin Books, 1985.

Mitchell, Tim. *Intoxicated Identities: Alcohol's Power in Mexican History and Culture*. London: Routledge, 2004.

Monterrubio, Carlos, Bharath Josiam, and Ana Pricila Sosa. "Spring Break's Social Impacts and Residents' Attitudes in Cancun, Mexico: A Qualitative Approach." *International Journal of Tourism Anthropology* 4, no. 2 (2015): 145–61.

Mount Gay Distillers Ltd. "Mount Gay Barbados Rum." Accessed February 17, 2017. https://www.mountgayrum.com/.

Myers-Boone, Leanne. "South Louisiana's Craft Distillery Boom." *Country Roads*, July 2, 2013.

Napier, I. A. "A Brief History of the Development of the Hardwood Industry in Belize." *Coedwigwr* 26 (1973): 36–43.

Nash, Dennison. 1995. "An Exploration of Tourism as Superstructure." In *Change in Tourism: People, Places, Processes*, edited by Richard W. Butler and Douglas G. Pearce, 30–46. London: Routledge, 1995.

National Oceanographic and Atmospheric Administration. "Easy to Read HUR-DAT 2008." Accessed April 18, 2018. http://www.aoml.noaa.gov/hrd/hurdat/easyread-2009.html.

Nemser, Daniel. "'To Avoid This Mixture': Rethinking Pulque in Colonial Mexico City." *Food and Foodways* 19, no. 1–2 (2011): 98–121.

Newman, T. Stell. "A Dating Key for Post-Eighteenth Century Bottles." *Historical Archaeology* 4 (1970): 70–75.

Nickel, Herbert J. *El Peonaje en las Haciendas Mexicanas: Interpretaciones, Fuentes, Hallazgos.* México, Distrito Federal: Universidad Iberoamericana, 1997.

Nicol, Denis A. "Rum." In *Fermented Beverage Production*, 263–87. New York: Springer, 2003.

Norris, Ruth, J. Scott Wilber, and Luís Oswaldo Morales Marín. "Community-Based Ecotourism in the Maya Forest: Problems and Potentials." In *Timber, Tourists, and Temples: Conservation and Development in the Maya Forest of Belize, Guatemala and México*, edited by Richard B. Primack, David Barton Bray, Hugo A. Galletti, and Ismael Pinciano, 328–42. Covelo, Calif.: Island Press, 1998.

Norton, Marcy. "Foreword." In *Substance and Seduction: Ingested Commodities in Early Modern Mesoamerica*, edited by Stacey Schwartzkopf and Kathryn E. Sampeck, vii–xiv. Austin: University of Texas Press, 2017.

Olcott, Henry S. *Sorgho and Imphee, the Chinese and African Sugar Canes: A Treatise Upon Their Origin, Varieties, and Culture; Their Value as a Forage Crop; and the Manufacture of Sugar, Syrup, Alcohol, Beer, Wines, Cider, Vinegar, Starch and Dye-Stuffs; with a Paper by Leonard Wray, Esq. of Caffaria, and Description of His Patented Process for Crystallizing the Juice of the Imphee, to Which Are Added Copious Translations of Valuable French Pamphlets.* New York: A. O. Moore, Agricultural Book Publishers, 1857.

Opie, Frederick Douglass. "Alcohol and Lowdown Culture in Caribbean Guatemala and Honduras, 1898–1922." In *Distilling the Influence of Alcohol: Aguardiente in Guatemalan History*, edited by David Carey Jr. Gainesville: University Press of Florida, 2012.

Owens, Bill, and Alan Dikty. "The Distilling Process." In *The Art of Distilling Whiskey and Other Spirits: An Enthusiast's Guide to the Artisan Distilling of Potent Potables*, edited by Bill Owens and Alan Dikty, 24–39. Bloomington, Ind.: Quarry Books, 2009.

Oxford African American Studies Center. "Jamaica." 2010. Accessed February 17, 2019. http://www.oxfordaasc.com/public/samples/sample_country.jsp.

Palka, Joel W. 2009. "Historical Archaeology of Indigenous Culture Change in Mesoamerica." *Journal of Archaeological Research* 17, no. 4 (2009): 297–346.

Palka, Joel W. *Unconquered Lacandon Maya: Ethnohistory and Archaeology of Indigenous Culture Change*. Gainesville: University Press of Florida, 2005.

Pang, Eul-Soo. "Modernization and Slavocracy in Nineteenth-Century Brazil." *Journal of Interdisciplinary History* 9, no. 4 (1979): 667–88.

Paredes, Alfonso. *Social Control of Drinking Among the Aztec Indians of Mesoamerica*. Piscataway, N.J.: Rutgers University Center for Alcohol Studies, 1975.

Parnell, J. Jacob, Richard E. Terry, and Charles Golden. "Using In-Field Phosphate Testing to Rapidly Identify Middens at Piedras Negras, Guatemala." *Geoarchaeology* 16 (2001): 855–73.

Patch, Robert W. 1985. "Agrarian Change in Eighteenth-Century Yucatán." *The Hispanic American Historical Review* 65 (1985): 21–49.

Patch, Robert W. "The (Almost) Forgotten Plants of Yucatán." In *The Lowland Maya Area: Three Millennia at the Human Wildlife Interface*, edited by Arturo Gomez-Pompa, Michael F. Allen, Scott L. Fedick, and Juan José Jimenez-Osornio, 561–69. New York: Food Products Press, 2003.

Patch, Robert W. *Maya and Spaniard in Yucatán, 1648–1812*. Stanford, Calif.: Stanford University Press, 1993.

Pelas, Holly Renee. "Tourism Development in Cancun, Mexico: An Analysis of State-Directed Tourism Initiatives in a Developing Nation." Master's thesis, Georgetown University, 2011.

Pezzarossi, Guido. "'Confites, Melcochas y Otras Golosinas . . . Muy Dañosas': Sugar, Alcohol, and Biopolitics in Colonial Guatemala." In *Substance and Seduction: Ingested Commodities in Early Modern Mesoamerica*, edited by Stacey Schwartzkopf and Kathryn E. Sampeck, 147–75. Austin: University of Texas Press, 2017.

Pierce, Gretchen, and Áurea Toxqui eds. *Alcohol in Latin America: A Social and Cultural History*. Tucson: University of Arizona Press, 2015.

Pi-Sunyer, Oriol, and Thomas R. Brooke. "Tourism, Environmentalism and Cultural Survival in Quintana Roo." In *Environmental Sociology: From Analysis to Action*, 43–72. Lanham, Md.: Rowman & Littlefield, 2005.

Pi-Sunyer, Oriel, and Thomas R. Brooke. "Tourism, Environmentalism, and Cultural Survival in Quintana Roo." In *Life and Death Matters: Human Rights and the Environment at the End of the Millennium*, edited by Barbara Rose Johnston, 187–212. Walnut Creek, Calif.: Alta Mira Press, 1997.

Pi-Sunyer, Oriol, and Thomas R. Brooke. "Tourism and the Transformation of Daily Life Along the Riviera Maya of Quintana Roo, Mexico." *Journal of Latin American and Caribbean Anthropology* 20, no. 1 (2015): 87–109.

Pi-Sunyer, Oriel, Thomas R. Brooke, and Magalí Daltabuit. "Tourism and Maya Society in Quintana Roo." In *Latin American Studies Consortium of New England, Occasional Paper No. 17.* Storrs, Conn.: Center for Latin American and Caribbean Studies, 1999.

Plant, Roger. *Sugar and Modern Slavery: A Tale of Two Countries.* London: Zed Books, 1987.

Rabelo, S. C., H. Carrere, R. Maciel Filho, and A. C. Costa. "Production of Bioethanol, Methane and Heat from Sugarcane Bagasse in a Biorefinery Concept." *Bioresource Technology* 102, no. 17 (2011): 7887–95.

Rajotte, Freda, ed. *Tourism: A New Type of Sugar.* Honolulu: University of Hawai'i, 1987.

Ratekin, Mervyn. "The Early Sugar Industry in Española." *Hispanic American Historical Review* 34, no. 1 (1954): 1–19.

Raymond, Nathaniel C. "Remembrance of Things Past: Hacendados and Ejidatarios in Yucatán, Mexico." *Human Organization* 36 (1977): 371–75.

Re Cruz, Alicia. "Milpas of Corn and Tourism Milpas." In *Lifeways in the Northern Maya Lowlands: New Approaches to Archaeology in the Yucatán Peninsula,* edited by Jennifer P. Mathews and Bethany A. Morrison, 210–20. Tucson: University of Arizona Press, 2005.

Re Cruz, Alicia. "The Thousand and One Faces of Cancun." *Urban Anthropology* 25, no. 3 (1996): 283–310.

Re Cruz, Alicia. *The Two Milpas of Chan Kom: Scenarios of a Maya Village Life.* Albany: State University of New York Press, 1996.

Redclift, Michael. *Chewing Gum: The Fortunes of Taste.* New York: Routledge, 2004.

Redfield, R., and A. Villa Rojas. *Chan Kom: A Maya Village.* Chicago: University of Chicago Press, 1962 [1934].

Reed, Nelson. *The Caste War of Yucatán.* Stanford, Calif.: Stanford University Press, 2001 [1964].

Reinhold, Robert, "Building Anew in the Yucatán." *New York Times,* February 26, 1989.

Rejón Patrón, Lourdes. *Hacienda Tabi: Un Capitulo en la Historia de Yucatán.* Vol. 3, *Cuadernos de Cultura Yucateca.* Mérida: Gobierno del Estado de Yucatán, 1993.

Remmers, Lawrence James. "Henequén, the Caste War and Economy of Yucatán, 1846–1883: The Roots of Dependence in a Mexican Region." PhD thesis, University of California at Los Angeles, 1981.

Rey, Pierre-Philippe. *Las Alianzas de Clases, Siglo XXI.* México, Distrito Federal: Siglo Veintiuno, 1976.

Richardson, Bonham C. *Caribbean Migrants: Environment and Human Survival on St. Kitts and Nevis.* Knoxville: University of Tennessee Press, 1983.

Riding, Alan. "México Drawing Foreign Hotels." *New York Times*, May 6, 1980.

Rioux, Nyle Lucien. "The Reign of 'King Henequen': The Rise and Fall of Yucatán's Export Crop from the Pre-Columbian Era through 1930." Master's thesis, Bates College, 2014.

Rivero, Piedad Peniche. "La Comunidad Doméstica de la Hacienda Henequenera de Yucatán, Mexico, 1870–1915." *Mexican Studies/Estudios Mexicanos* 15 (1999): 1–33.

Rivero, Piedad Peniche. "La Demografía de la Nohoch Cuenta en las Haciendas Henequeras y Pueblos del Municipio de Umán, Yucatán, México, Durante el Porfiriato." *Mexicon* 20, no. 2 (1998): 32–36.

Rivero, Piedad Peniche. "Gender, Bridewealth, and Marriage: Social Reproduction of Peons on Henequen Haciendas in Yucatán (1870–1901)." In *Women of the Mexican Countryside, 1850–1900: Creating Spaces, Shaping Transitions*, edited by Heather Fowler-Salamini, 74–92. Tucson: University of Arizona Press, 1994.

Rivero, Piedad Peniche. *La Historia Secreta de la Hacienda Henequenera de Yucatán: Deudas, Migración y Resistencia Maya, 1879–1915.* Mérida: Archivo General de la Nación y Instituto de Cultura de Yucatán, 2010.

Rivero, Piedad Peniche. "From Milpero and Lunero to Henequenero; A Transition to Capitalism in Yucatán, Mexico." In *The Lowland Maya Area: Three Millennia at the Human Wildlife Interface*, edited by Gómez-Pompa, Arturo, Michael F. Allen, Scott L. Fedick, and Juan José Jiménez-Osornio, 571–84. New York: Food Products Press, 2003.

Robinson, David J. "La Historia Secreta de la Hacienda Henequenera de Yucatán: Deudas, Migración y Resistencia Maya (1879–1915) (review)." *Journal of Latin American Geography* 10, no. 1 (2011): 212–13.

Rodrigue, John C. "Labor Militancy and Black Grassroots Political Mobilization in the Louisiana Sugar Region, 1865–1868." *Journal of Southern History* 67, no. 1 (2001): 115–42.

Rodríguez O., Jaime E. *We Are Now the True Spaniards: Sovereignty, Revolution, Independence, and the Emergence of the Federal Republic of Mexico, 1808–1824.* Stanford: Stanford University Press, 2012.

Rogers, Thomas D. *The Deepest Wounds: A Labor and Environmental History of Sugar in Northeast Brazil.* Chapel Hill: University of North Carolina Press, 2010.

Rogoziński, Jan. *A Brief History of the Caribbean: From the Arawak and the Carib to the Present.* New York: Facts on File, 1999.

Rothers, Larry. "México Looks to a Second Acapulco." *New York Times*, December 20, 1988.

Rugeley, Terry. *Rebellion Now and Forever: Mayas, Hispanics, and Caste War Violence in Yucatán, 1800–1880*. Stanford, Calif.: Stanford University Press, 2009.

Rugeley, Terry. *Yucatán's Maya Peasantry and the Origins of the Caste War*. Arlington: University of Texas Press, 1996.

Rugemer, Edward, B. "The Development of Mastery and Race in the Comprehensive Slave Codes of the Greater Caribbean during the Seventeenth Century." *The William and Mary Quarterly* 70, no. 3 (2013): 429–58.

Rum Ratings. 2018. "Edwin Charley." Accessed February 17, 2019. https://www.rumratings.com/companies/347-edwin-charley-rum.

Russell, Sarah. "Intermarriage and Intermingling: Constructing the Planter Class in Louisiana's Sugar Parishes, 1803–1850." *Louisiana History* 46, no. 4 (2005): 407–34.

Rutledge, Raquel. "140 Victims of Mexico Resort Blackouts. Now, Congress Wants Action." *Milwaukee Journal Sentinel*, February 13, 2018.

Said, Edward. *Orientalism*. London: Routledge, 1978.

Sanchez, Delia, Tiffany A. Whittaker, Emma Hamilton, and Sarah Arango. "Familial Ethnic Socialization, Gender Role Attitudes, and Ethnic Identity Development in Mexican-Origin Early Adolescents." *Cultural Diversity and Ethnic Minority Psychology* 23 (2017): 335–47.

Satchell, Veront M. "Estate Ruins as Loci for Industrial Archaeology in Jamaica." *Industrial Archaeology Review* 26, no. 1 (2004): 37–44.

Savage, Melissa. "Ecological Disturbance and Nature Tourism." *Geographical Review* 83, no. 3 (2004): 290–300.

Scarpaci, Jean Ann. "Immigrants in the New South: Italians in Louisiana's Sugar Parishes, 1880–1910." *Labor History* 16, no. 2 (1975): 165–83.

Schwartz, Norman B. *Forest Society: A Social History of Petén, Guatemala*. Philadelphia: University of Pennsylvania Press, 1990.

Schwartzkopf, Stacey. "Consumption, Custom, and Control: Aguardiente in Nineteenth Century Maya Guatemala." In *Distilling the Influence of Alcohol: Aguardiente in Guatemalan History*, edited by David Carey Jr., 17–41. Gainesville: University Press of Florida, 2012.

Schwartzkopf, Stacey, and Kathryn E. Sampeck. "Introduction: Consuming Desires in Mesoamerica." In *Substance and Seduction: Ingested Commodities in Early Modern Mesoamerica*, edited by Stacey Schwartzkopf and Kathryn E. Sampeck, 1–24. Austin: University of Texas Press, 2017.

Scott, James C. *Weapons of the Weak: Everyday Forms of Peasant Resistance*. New Haven: Yale University Press, 1985.

Shabelnik, Tatiana, Chuck Thomas, Elaine Smyth, and Matt Mullenix. "Sugar at LSU: A Chronology." Accessed February 17, 2019. https://www.lib.lsu.edu/sites/all/files/sc/exhibits/e-exhibits/sugar/contents.html.

Sheller, M. "The New Caribbean Complexity: Mobility Systems, Tourism and Spatial Rescaling." *Singapore Journal of Tropical Geography* 30 (2009): 189–203.

Sheridan, Richard B. "The Plantation Revolution and the Industrial Revolution, 1625–1775." *Caribbean Studies* 9, no. 3 (1969): 5–25.

Sheridan, Richard B. *Sugar and Slavery: An Economic History of the British West Indies, 1623–1775.* Baltimore: Johns Hopkins University Press, 1974.

Shuler, Kristina Andrea. "Health, History, and Sugar: A Bioarchaeological Study of Enslaved Africans from Newton Plantation, Barbados, West Indies." PhD thesis, Southern Illinois University, Carbondale, 2005.

Sieder, Rachel. "'Paz, Progreso, Justicia Y Honradez': Law and Citizenship in Alta Verapaz During the Regime of Jorge Ubico." *Bulletin of Latin American Research* 19, no. 3 (2000): 283–302.

Smith, Adam. *The Wealth of Nations.* New York: Modern Library, 1937.

Smith, Frederick H. "Alcohol, Slavery, and African Cultural Continuity in the British Caribbean." In *Drinking: Anthropological Approaches*, edited by Igor de Garine and Valerie de Garine, 212–24. New York: Berghahn Books, 2001.

Smith, Frederick H. *The Archaeology of Alcohol and Drinking.* Gainesville: University Press of Florida, 2008.

Smith, Frederick H., and Karl Watson. "Urbanity, Sociability, and Commercial Exchange in the Barbados Sugar Trade: A Comparative Colonial Archaeological Perspective on Bridgetown, Barbados in the Seventeenth Century." *International Journal of Historical Archaeology* 13, no. 1 (2009): 63–79.

Smout, Thomas C. "The Early Scottish Sugar Houses, 1660-1720." *The Economic History Review* 14, no. 2 (1961): 240–53.

Snook, Laura K. "Sustaining Harvests of Mahogany (Swietenia Macrophylla King) from Mexico's Yucatán Forests: Past, Present, and Future." In *Timber, Tourists, and Temples: Conservation and Development in the Maya Forest of Belize, Guatemala, and Mexico*, edited by Richard B. Primack, David Barton Bray, Hugo A. Gallettii, and Ismael Ponciano, 61–80. Washington D.C.: Island Press, 1998.

Solomon, S. "Post-harvest Deterioration of Sugarcane." *Sugar Tech* 11, no. 2 (2009): 109–23.

Standing, Guy. *A Precariat Charter: From Denizens to Citizens.* London: Bloomsbury, 2014.

Statista "Sugar Cane Production in the U.S. from 2010 to 2017, by State (in 1,000 tons)." Accessed February 17, 2019. https://www.statista.com/statistics/191975/sugarcane-production-in-the-us-by-state/.

Stern, Alexandra Minna. "Responsible Mothers and Normal Children: Eugenics, Nationalism, and Welfare in Post-Revolutionary Mexico, 1920–1940." *Journal of Historical Sociology* 12, no. 4 (1999): 369–97.

Stockton, William. "México Pushes Tourism Anew." *New York Times*, April 27, 1986.

Stronza, Amanda. "Anthropology of Tourism: Forging New Ground for Ecotourism and Other Alternatives." *Annual Review of Anthropology* 30 (2001): 261–83.

Stross, Brian. "The Mexican Cantina as a Setting for Interaction." *Kroeber Anthropological Society Papers* 37 (1967): 58–89.

Sullivan, Paul R. *Para que Lucharon los Mayas Rebeldes, y Vida y Muerte de Bernardino Cen.* Chetumal, Quintana Roo: Universidad de Quintana Roo, 1998.

Sullivan, Paul R. *Unfinished Conversations: Mayas and Foreigners Between Two Wars.* Oakland: University of California Press, 1991.

Sullivan, Paul R. *Xuxub Must Die: The Lost Histories of a Murder on the Yucatán.* Pittsburgh: University of Pittsburgh Press, 2004.

Sweitz, Samuel R. "A Historical Outline of Hacienda San Juan Bautista Tabi." *Contributions to Global Historical Archaeology* 3 (2012a): 77–87.

Sweitz, Samuel R. "On the Periphery of the Periphery: Household Archaeology at Hacienda Tabi, Yucatán, Mexico." PhD thesis, Texas A&M University, 2005.

Sweitz, Sam R. "Total History: The Meaning of Hacienda Tabi." In *On the Periphery of the Periphery*, 239–51. New York: Springer, 2012b.

Takaki, Ronald T. *Pau Hana: Plantation Life and Labor in Hawaii, 1835–1920.* Honolulu, University of Hawai'i Press, 1984.

Takeguchi, J., W. Hollyer, M. Koga, K. Hakoda, K. Rohrbach, H. C. S. Bittenbender, B. Buckley, et al. "History of Sugar." In *History of Agriculture in Hawaii.* Honolulu: Government of Hawai'i, 1999.

Tanenbaum, David J. "Trampling Paradise: Dream Vacation—Environmental Nightmare?" *Environmental Health Perspectives* 108, no. 5 (2000): A214–19.

Taube, Karl A. "Ancient and Contemporary Maya Conceptions About Field and Forest." In *The Lowland Maya Area: Three Millennia at the Human Wildlife Interface*, edited by Arturo Gómez-Pompa, Michael F. Allen, Scott L. Fedick, and Juan José Jiménez-Osornio, 461–94. New York: Food Products Press, 2003.

Taylor, William B. *Drinking, Homicide, and Rebellion in Colonial Mexican Villages.* Palo Alto, Calif.: Stanford University Press, 1979.

Teclemariam, Tammie. "How Haiti Is Making Some of the Best Rum on Earth." *Wine Enthusiast Magazine*, 2018. Accessed February 17, 2019. https://www.winemag.com/2018/04/12/haiti-clairin-rum/.

Terry, Thomas Philip. *Terry's Mexico: Handbook for Travellers.* Mexico City: Sonora News Company, 1909.

Thyme Machine Cuisine. "The Origins of Rum, and Its Place in History." Accessed February 17, 2019. https://www.thymemachinecuisine.com/single-post/2017/09/20/the-origins-of-rum-and-its-place-in-history.

Torres, Rebecca. "Cancun's Tourism Development from a Fordist Spectrum of Analysis." *Tourist Studies* 2 (2002a): 87–116.

Torres, Rebecca. "Linkages Between Tourism and Agriculture in Quintana Roo, Mexico." PhD thesis, University of California, Davis, 2000.

Torres, Rebecca, and Janet Henshall Momsen. "Challenges and Potential for Linking Tourism and Agriculture to Achieve Pro-poor Tourism Objectives." *Progress in Development Studies* 4, no. 4 (2004): 294–318.

Torres, Rebecca, and Janet Henshall Momsen. "Gringolandia: Cancun and the American Tourist." In *Adventures into Mexico: American Tourism Beyond the Border*, edited by Nicholas Dagen Bloom, 58–73. Lanham, Md.: Rowman & Littlefield, 2006.

Torres, Rebecca Maria. "Toward a Better Understanding of Tourism and Agriculture Linkages in the Yucatán: Tourist Food Consumption and Preferences." *Tourism Geographies* 4, no. 3 (2002b): 282–306.

Torres, Rebecca Maria, and Janet D. Momsen. 2005. "Gringolandia: The Construction of a New Tourist Space in Mexico." *Annals of the Association of American Geographers* 95, no. 2 (2005): 314–35.

Toxqui, Áurea. "Women's Involvement in the Pulquería World of Mexico City: 1850–1910." In *Alcohol in Latin America: A Social and Cultural History*, edited by Gretchen Pierce and Áurea Toxqui, 104–30. Tucson: University of Arizona Press, 2014.

Tozzer, Alfred. *A Comparative Study of the Mayas and the Lacandones*. New York: McMillan Company, 1907.

Turner, John Kenneth. *Barbarous Mexico*. Chicago: Charles H. Kerr & Company, 1969 [1911].

Tyson, George F. "'Our Side': Caribbean Immigrant Labourers and the Transition to Free Labour on St. Croix, 1849–79." In *Small Islands, Large Questions: Society, Culture and Resistance in the Post-Emancipation Caribbean*, edited by Karen Fog Olwig, 135–60. London: Frank Cass, 1995.

Ultimate Rum Guide. "Dominican Republic." *Ultimate Rum Guide*. Accessed February 17, 2010. http://ultimaterumguide.com/dominican-republic/.

Valenzuela Zapata, Ana Guadalupe, and Gary Paul Nabhan. *Tequila: A Natural and Cultural History*. Tucson: University of Arizona Press, 2003.

Vassallo-Oby, Christine. 2010. "Circulation and Consumption: Transnational Mass Tourism in Cancun, Mexico." *Student Anthropologist* 2, no. 1 (2010): 38–45.

Vaughn, David. "Tourism and Biodiversity: A Convergence of Interests?" *International Affairs* 76, no. 2 (2000): 283–97.

Villalobos González, Martha H. "Las Concesiones Forestales en Quintana Roo a Fines del Porfiriato." *Relaciónes: Estudios de Historia y Sociedad* 14, no. 53 (1987): 87–112.

Villanueva Mukul, Eric, Armando Barta Verges, Marco Bellingery Martini, Ivan Franco Caceres, Jose Fernandez Souza, Arcadio Sabido Mendez, Jorge

Tomas Vera Pren, Roberto Escalante Semerena, and Francisco Hernandez Sosa. "Caracteristicas de la Produccion Durante el Porfiriato: 1876–1910." In *El Henequén en Yucatán: Industria, Mercado y Campesinos*, 78–89. Mérida: Maldonado Editores, 1990.

Vivanco, Luis A. "Certifying Sustainable Tourism in Costa Rica: Environmental Governance and Accountability in a Transitional Era." In *Central America in the New Millennium: Living Transition and Reimagining Democracy*, edited by J. L. Burrell and E. Moodie, 212–26. New York: Berghahn Books, 2013.

Vogt, Evan. *Zinancantan: A Maya Community in the Highlands of Chiapas*. Cambridge: The Belknap Press of Harvard University Press, 1969.

Vogt, John. *Portuguese Rule on the Gold Coast 1469–1682*. Athens: University of Georgia Press, 1979.

Wayne, Lucy B. *Sweet Cane: The Architecture of the Sugar Works of East Florida*. Tuscaloosa: University of Alabama Press, 2010.

Wells, Allen. "All in the Family: Railroads and Henequen Monoculture in Porfirian Yucatán." *The Hispanic American Historical Review* 72, no. 2 (1992): 159–209.

Wells, Allen. "Yucatán: Violence and Social Control on Henequen Plantations." In *Other Mexicos: Essays on Regional Mexican History*, edited by T. Benjamin and W. McNellie, 213–41. Albuquerque: University of New Mexico Press, 1984.

Wells, Allen. *Yucatán's Gilded Age: Haciendas, Henequen, and International Harvester*. Albuquerque: University of New Mexico Press, 1985.

Wells, Allen, and Gilbert M. Joseph. *Summer of Discontent, Seasons of Upheaval: Elite Politics and Rural Insurgency in Yucatán, 1876–1915*. Stanford, Calif.: Stanford University Press 1996.

Wilkinson, Alec. *Big Sugar: Seasons in the Cane Fields of Florida*. New York: Knopf, 1989.

Williams, Ian. *Rum: A Social and Sociable History of the Real Spirit of 1776*. New York: Nation Books, 2005.

Witt, Stephen F., Michael Z. Brook, and Peter J. Buckley. *The Management of International Tourism*. London: Unwin Hyman, 1991.

Wolf, Eric R. "Aspects of Group Relations in a Complex Society: Mexico." *American Anthropologist* 58, no. 6 (1956): 1065–78.

Wolf, Eric R., and Sidney W. Mintz. "Haciendas and Plantations in Middle America and the Antilles." *Social and Economic Studies* 6, no. 3 (1957): 380–412.

Wright, Amie. "'La Bebida Nacional': Pulque and Mexicanidad, 1920–46." *Canadian Journal of History* 44, no. 1 (2009): 1–24.

Xacur, Juan A., and Nicolás Lizama Cornelio (Colinas). *La Verdadera Historieta De Quintana Roo*. Chetumal, México: Dante, 1989.

Yaeger, Jason, Minette C. Church, Richard M. Leventhal, and Jennifer L. Dornan. "The San Pedro Maya Project: Preliminary Report of the 2001 Field Season." Submitted to the Belize Department of Archaeology, Belmopan, Belize, 2002.

Zavala, Silvio A. "La Encomienda Indiana." *El Trimestre Económico* 2, no. 8 (1935): 423–51.

Zavala, Silvio A. "Orígenes Coloniales del Peonaje en México." *El Trimestre Economico* 10, (1944): 711–48.

Zizumbo-Villarreal, Daniel, Fernando González-Zozaya, Angeles Olay-Barrientos, Laura Almendros-López, Patricia Flores-Pérez, and Patricia Colunga-GarcíaMarín. "Distillation in Western Mesoamerica Before European Contact." *Economic Botany* 63, no. 4 (2009): 413–26.

# INDEX

abolition: of debt peonage, 60; of encomienda system, 40; of hacienda system, 60; of slavery, 16, 19, 33, 34, 127n106

Africa: and religion, 37; and slavery, 3, 14, 33; and slaves in Barbados, 13–14, 24; and slaves in the Caribbean, 36; and slaves in Hawaii, 21, 34; and slaves in South America, 36; and sugar production, 10; and U.S. colonists trading rum for slaves, 10–11, 124n13

agriculture: and agribusiness, 18, 42; and workers, 34; cycles, 57; estates, 28–29; in Yucatan, 41–42, 43, 44, 48, 61, 134n42, 139n21; lands, 15; products, 5; schedules, 31; systems, 3

aguardiente: and debt, 98, 113, 116; and rituals, 95, 97; as import, 115; as social control, 98–99; as escape, 107, 112; as source of conflict, 96, 113; bans of, 42, 105, 116; criticism of, 37, 97; in Brazil, 12; in Guatemala, 100; in Yucatán, 5, 37, 42, 95, 113, 115, 116, 133n26; served to children, 37, 97. *See also* alcohol, cachaça

alcohol: and ritual, 12, 36, 37, 92, 96, 97, 136n94; and social control, 37, 91, 99, 105, 113, 132n111; and tourism, 92; and violence, 6, 104, 105, 113; bottles, 77, 85, 86, 89, 142n107; consumption, 8, 77, 95, 98, 102; content, 6, 19, 28, 94, 105, 143n6; imports, 12; on election day, 8, 111; in the pre-contact period, 92–95; in the post-contact period, 134n48; production, 12, 28, 65, 90, 91, 106, 114; produced illic-itly, 22, 96, 104, 106, 126n39; prohibition, 13, 22, 99, 114. *See also* aguardiente, balché, bootlegging, cachaça, pulque

alcoholism: among Indigenous peoples, 22, 61, 91, 92, 98, 104–105, 113, 114, 145n32; and stereotypes of the "drunken Indian," 97, 113

archaeological: data, 81; investigations, 63; invisibility, 5–6; practitioners of, 50, 68, 77, 108; records, 55, 70; sites, 111; theory, 137n135

archive: Archivo General en Yucatán (AGEY), 81, 142n83; documents, 68; research, 36; sources, 6

armies, 45, 61, 64, 123n12, 138n147. *See also* military

artifacts: analysis, 69, 140n43; and phosphate analysis, 140n48; assemblage, 73, 77, 120–122; density, 143n100; frequencies, 89; of glass, 77, 85, 86–88; of metal, 6, 78, 85, 87–88, 90; on soil surface, 71, 73, 85, 140n44; related to building materials, 76; related to subsistence, 77, 85, 89, 120–121, 140, 143

balché: and ritual, 92, 95; production 94–95; tree, 94, 95, 144n10. *See also* alcohol

Barbados: and slavery, 13, 14, 24, 36; colonization of, 13; geography of, 14, 32; rum production, 3, 13, 19, 126n49, 144n20; sugar production, 9, 19, 32

bars, 92, 96, 114, 116, 117. *See also* cantinas, taverns

from alcohol, 91; from weddings, 55;
multi-generational, 55, 136n114; of
children, 97; of foreign workers, 56; of
Urcelay family, 67; peonage definition, 44; peonage in Belize, 128n108;
peonage in Yucatán, 3–4, 23–24, 30,
32, 38–39, 42, 43, 50–54, 116; restricting
freedoms of workers, 4, 5, 24, 37, 44–45,
48, 54, 90, 98, 106; through scrip, 56;
*See also* scrip, tokens.
Decauville railroad, 81, 83, 85, 117. *See also*
railroad, train
Díaz, Porfirio, 48, 57, 79
distillation: equipment, 14, 28; experience,
28; independent, 19; in India, 127n106; in
pre-contact Mesoamerica, 124n19, 143n4;
of rum, 5, 6, 14, 16; processes, 23, 28, 92
distilled: alcohol, 37, 92, 96; rum, 96, 116;
spirits, 22, 94
distillery, 12, 14, 16, 23, 27, 80, 130n38; building, 76, 78, 89; craft, 108; equipment, 73,
76; in Barbados, 19; in Hawaii, 22; in
Yucatán, 23, 38, 73, 79, 108; of France, 27
domestic violence, 7, 33, 51, 104–105, 106,
143n1. *See also* drunkenness, violence
Dominican Republic: as Santo Domingo,
11, 15, 17; colonization in, 10; economy,
36; gold mines in, 10; Haitains in, 17,
33; rum in, 3; semi-coerced labor in, 17;
sugar in, 3, 36
drunkenness: and cantinas, 103; and
violence, 8, 55, 94, 95, 104, 143n1; as a
stereotype of Indigenous peoples, 97,
98; as an act of resistance, 38, 59, 65; as
mitigating factor in crime, 37, 38, 105;
and ritual, 97, 113; criticism of, 37, 98, 104,
105–106, 113, 130n32; punishment for, 21,
38, 94, 104. *See also* cantinas, domestic
violence, violence
Dry Law, 90, 105, 114. *See also* laws

economic: benefits to women, 106; elites,
48; hardship, 106; influence, 33; instability, 45; mobility, 33; prerequisites, 44;
restrictions on workers, 22, 36
economy: and tourism, 117; household,
56; of Barbados, 13; of Brazil, 12, 18; of
Cuba, 15, 42; of the Caribbean, 8, 60; of
Dominican Republic, 36; of Haiti, 11–12;

of Jamaica, 14, 19; of Quintana Roo, 90,
91, 106; of Veracruz, 42; of Yucatán, 6, 7,
44–45, 48, 60–61, 64, 91, 113; tied to rum,
96, 106, 115, 116; world, 3, 40, 73
ejido, 61, 62, 66, 139n21, 141n72. *See also* farm
El Cuyo (La Compania Agricola del Cuyo
y Anexas), 78–79, 81, 82, 142n82, 142n93
employee: conditions, 17, 50, 52, 57; female,
102–103, 104; harassment, 20; in tourism,
8, 107–108; low-skill, 109; skilled, 57;
transportation, 8
employer: abuses, 4, 21, 37, 90, 139n32; benefits, 17, 61; coercion, 3, 22, 52; loans, 4, 44;
perspectives, 4
encomienda: in Yucatan, 63; of Montejo
family, 13, 41, 115; system, 40, 133n4,
133n13 European: agriculture, 31;
alcoholism, 98; colonies, 4, 31; conquest,
92, 95, 115, 124n19, 144n7; diseases, 63;
distilled alcohol, 37; elites, 91; empire, 13;
encomienda system, 40; goods, 134n48;
hacienda owners, 113; laborers, 3, 24, 32;
oppression, 47; rum, 31, 96; slavery, 18;
sugar, 3, 10, 11, 18; sugar beets, 18; sugar
imports, 27, 31, 60; taverns, 99; travel, 60

family: and alcohol, 96, 104, 106; and
enslavement cycles, 24; and marriage
arrangements, 55, 96–97; and migration
to Cancun, 110; and the role of women,
102, 104, 106; cycles of debt, 5, 29–30,
44, 52, 53, 91, 98; encomienda grant,
13, 41, 115, 133n13; evictions of, 19–20;
income, 116; labor requirements, 45,
50, 55, 56, 57; land-grants, 41; living on
haciendas, 70, 77, 91; run-plantations,
18; Urcelay, 66, 67, 123; violence, 8, 55,
104, 113; wages, 56; wealth, 32, 66
farm: cattle-, 91; crops, 41; communal, 116;
factory-, 29, 51, 123n6; fields, 47, 65;
foreman, 131n58; henequen, 61; land,
4, 14, 32, 41, 43, 61, 62, 126n44; milpa,
134n33; owner, 19; schedule, 31; subsis-
tence-, 31; sugarcane, 115; workers, 59.
*See also* ejido, milpa
farmers, 13, 18, 33, 41, 48, 53, 59
fermentation: drink, 125n18; liquid, 79, 94;
process, 27, 28; tank, 27, 69, 70, 73, 79,
141n77

# ABOUT THE AUTHORS

**John R. Gust** is the lab director and a principal investigator at Cogstone Resource Management in Orange, California. *Sugarcane and Rum* is the culmination of research started in 2009 and draws on research that began in 2001.

**Jennifer P. Mathews** is a professor of anthropology at Trinity University in San Antonio and has conducted research studying the ancient, historic, and contemporary Maya in the Yucatán Peninsula of México since 1993.